CERTIFIED WEB DEVELOPER
NOVICE TO NINJA

HTML, CSS AND JAVASCRIPT

3 BOOKS IN 1

BOOK 1
HTML ESSENTIALS: BUILDING BLOCKS OF THE WEB

BOOK 2
MASTERING CSS: STYLING TECHNIQUES FOR
PROFESSIONAL WEB DESIGN

BOOK 3
JAVASCRIPT WIZARDRY: ADVANCED TECHNIQUES
FOR DYNAMIC WEB DEVELOPMENT

ROB BOTWRIGHT

Published by Rob Botwright
Library of Congress Cataloging-in-Publication Data
ISBN 978-1-83938-725-8
Cover design by Rizzo

Disclaimer

The contents of this book are based on extensive research and the best available historical sources. However, the author and publisher make no claims, promises, or guarantees about the accuracy, completeness, or adequacy of the information contained herein. The information in this book is provided on an "as is" basis, and the author and publisher disclaim any and all liability for any errors, omissions, or inaccuracies in the information or for any actions taken in reliance on such information. The opinions and views expressed in this book are those of the author and do not necessarily reflect the official policy or position of any organization or individual mentioned in this book. Any reference to specific people, places, or events is intended only to provide historical context and is not intended to defame or malign any group, individual, or entity. The information in this book is intended for educational and entertainment purposes only. It is not intended to be a substitute for professional advice or judgment. Readers are encouraged to conduct their own research and to seek professional advice where appropriate. Every effort has been made to obtain necessary permissions and acknowledgments for all images and other copyrighted material used in this book. Any errors or omissions in this regard are unintentional, and the author and publisher will correct them in future editions.

BOOK 1: HTML ESSENTIALS: BUILDING BLOCKS OF THE WEB

Introduction 5
Chapter 1: Introduction to HTML: Understanding the Structure.. 8
Chapter 2: Basic Tags and Elements: Getting Started with HTML 15
Chapter 3: Formatting Text and Images 22
Chapter 4: Creating Hyperlinks and Anchors.. 31
Chapter 5: Lists and Tables: Organizing Content 39
Chapter 6: Forms and Input Elements: User Interaction... 47
Chapter 7: Semantic HTML: Enhancing Accessibility and SEO 56
Chapter 8: Multimedia Integration: Adding Audio and Video 68
Chapter 9: CSS Fundamentals: Styling Your HTML 78
Chapter 10: Responsive Design: Adapting to Different Devices.. 89
Chapter 11: HTML5 Features and Modern Practices 98
Chapter 12: Best Practices and Next Steps in HTML Development.. 106

BOOK 2 - MASTERING CSS: STYLING TECHNIQUES FOR PROFESSIONAL WEB DESIGN

Chapter 1: Understanding the Box Model.. 113
Chapter 2: Selectors and Specificity.. 122
Chapter 3: Cascading and Inheritance... 131
Chapter 4: Working with Typography.. 139
Chapter 5: Styling Links and Navigation 147
Chapter 6: Layouts with Flexbox... 155
Chapter 7: Grid Systems for Advanced Layouts.. 163
Chapter 8: Responsive Design with Media Queries 172
Chapter 9: Transformations and Transitions... 180
Chapter 10: Animations and Keyframes 188
Chapter 11: Customizing Forms and Inputs 197
Chapter 12: Optimization and Performance in CSS 206

BOOK 3 - JAVASCRIPT WIZARDRY: ADVANCED TECHNIQUES FOR DYNAMIC WEB DEVELOPMENT

Chapter 1: Introduction to JavaScript: Language Fundamentals... 215
Chapter 2: Working with Variables and Data Types... 223
Chapter 3: Control Flow: Conditionals and Loops... 230
Chapter 4: Functions and Scope 235
Chapter 5: Arrays and Objects: Complex Data Structures 241
Chapter 6: DOM Manipulation: Interacting with HTML 248
Chapter 7: Events and Event Handling... 255
Chapter 8: Asynchronous JavaScript: Promises and Callbacks... 261
Chapter 9: AJAX and Fetch API: Making HTTP Requests... 269
Chapter 10: Error Handling and Debugging Techniques 276
Chapter 11: Advanced JavaScript Patterns and Best Practices... 283
Chapter 12: Building Dynamic Web Applications: Real-World Projects 291
Conclusion 300

Introduction

Introducing the ultimate learning resource for aspiring web developers - the "Certified Web Developer: Novice To Ninja" book bundle. This comprehensive bundle consists of three essential volumes: "HTML Essentials: Building Blocks of the Web," "Mastering CSS: Styling Techniques for Professional Web Design," and "JavaScript Wizardry: Advanced Techniques for Dynamic Web Development."

In today's digital age, a strong foundation in HTML, CSS, and JavaScript is indispensable for anyone looking to pursue a career in web development. Whether you're a novice eager to embark on your coding journey or an experienced developer seeking to level up your skills, this bundle has you covered.

Book 1, "HTML Essentials," serves as your gateway into the world of web development. Learn how to create the structural framework of websites using HTML, understand the importance of semantic markup, and master the essential elements that form the backbone of every web page.

Book 2, "Mastering CSS," takes your web design skills to the next level. Dive deep into the realm of Cascading Style Sheets and discover advanced styling techniques that will transform your web pages into visually stunning masterpieces. From responsive design principles to flexbox and grid layouts, this book equips you with the tools to create professional-grade designs.

Book 3, "JavaScript Wizardry," unlocks the power of dynamic web development. Explore the intricacies of JavaScript, from manipulating the Document Object Model (DOM) to handling asynchronous operations and implementing cutting-edge frameworks. Whether you're building interactive user interfaces or crafting feature-rich web applications, this book will guide you through advanced techniques and best practices.

With the "Certified Web Developer: Novice To Ninja" book bundle, you'll not only gain a comprehensive understanding of HTML, CSS, and JavaScript but also acquire the skills and knowledge needed to excel in the competitive field of web development. Whether you're aiming to kickstart your career or elevate your expertise to ninja-level status, this bundle is your ultimate companion on the journey to becoming a certified web developer.

BOOK 1
HTML ESSENTIALS
BUILDING BLOCKS OF THE WEB

ROB BOTWRIGHT

Chapter 1: Introduction to HTML: Understanding the Structure

The evolution of HTML traces back to the early days of the World Wide Web when Tim Berners-Lee conceived the idea of a markup language for sharing documents across different computer systems. Initially, HTML was a simple language designed to structure and format text-based documents, with tags like <b> for bold and <i> for italics. However, as the web grew in popularity and complexity, HTML underwent significant transformations to accommodate the changing needs of web developers and users alike. With the release of HTML 2.0 in 1995, the language gained standardized features like forms and tables, laying the foundation for more interactive web experiences. This version also introduced the <img> tag for embedding images, further enriching web content.

HTML continued to evolve rapidly with the emergence of the browser wars in the late 1990s, as browser vendors competed to introduce new features and capabilities. HTML 3.2, released in 1997, brought significant enhancements such as support for tables, frames, and image maps, enabling developers to create more complex layouts and interactive elements. This version also marked the beginning of the era of dynamic HTML (DHTML), allowing for dynamic content manipulation through scripting languages like JavaScript.

As the demand for richer web applications grew, the need for a more powerful and extensible markup language became evident. This led to the development of HTML 4.01, released in 1999, which introduced features like cascading style sheets (CSS) for precise control over the presentation of web pages, as well as support for multimedia elements through the <audio> and <video> tags. HTML 4.01 also standardized the use of scripting languages like JavaScript for client-side interactivity, paving the way for the modern web applications we use today.

With the dawn of the new millennium came the era of web standards and the formation of the World Wide Web Consortium (W3C), the organization responsible for overseeing the development of HTML and other web technologies. HTML underwent a major overhaul with the release of XHTML 1.0 in 2000, which aimed to bring the language closer to the rules of XML while maintaining backward compatibility with HTML 4.01. XHTML introduced stricter syntax rules and emphasized the separation of content from presentation, laying the groundwork for a more semantic and accessible web.

However, the adoption of XHTML faced challenges due to its stricter syntax and the complexity of transitioning existing HTML codebases. This led to the development of HTML5, the latest major revision of the HTML standard, which was designed to address the shortcomings of XHTML while introducing new features to support the modern web ecosystem. HTML5, released in 2014, introduced a plethora of new elements and attributes for multimedia, graphics, and interactive content, including <canvas> for drawing graphics dynamically, <audio> and <video> for embedding media, and <svg> for scalable vector graphics.

HTML5 also brought significant improvements in the areas of semantics, accessibility, and offline web applications, with new elements like <header>, <footer>, <nav>, and <article> providing semantic meaning to web content, and features like localStorage and Web Storage API enabling web applications to store data locally for offline use. Additionally, HTML5 introduced the concept of web components, allowing developers to create reusable custom elements with encapsulated functionality, further enhancing the modularity and maintainability of web applications.

Today, HTML continues to evolve with ongoing efforts to standardize new features and improve existing ones through the HTML Living Standard, a continuously updated specification maintained by the W3C. The evolution of HTML reflects the ever-changing nature of the web and the constant push for innovation and improvement in web technologies. From its humble beginnings as a simple markup language to its current status as the foundation of the modern web, HTML has come a long way, shaping the way we create, share, and interact with information online.

An HTML document serves as the backbone of web content, providing structure and formatting instructions that browsers use to render web pages. Understanding the anatomy of an HTML document is essential for web developers to create well-structured and accessible websites. At the core of every HTML document is the HTML element, denoted by the opening <html> tag and closing </html> tag, which encloses all other elements on the page and defines it as an HTML document. Within the HTML element, the <head> element contains metadata and links to external resources, such as stylesheets and scripts, that are essential for the presentation and functionality of the web page. To create a new HTML document from scratch, developers can use a text editor like Visual Studio Code or Sublime Text and save the file with a .html extension, ensuring that it adheres to the HTML standard.

Moving on, the <title> element, nested within the <head> element, specifies the title of the web page, which appears in the browser's title bar or tab. This title serves as a concise descriptor of the page's content and is crucial for search engine optimization (SEO) and user experience. Another important element within the <head> section is the <meta> element, which provides metadata about the HTML document, such as the character encoding, viewport settings, and author information. Including appropriate meta tags can improve the accessibility and performance of the web page across different devices and browsers.

In addition to metadata, the <head> section may contain references to external resources, such as stylesheets and scripts, using the <link> and <script> elements, respectively. For example, developers can link an external CSS stylesheet to the HTML document using the <link> element with the rel attribute set to "stylesheet" and the href attribute pointing to the location of the stylesheet file. Similarly, JavaScript files can be included in the HTML document using the <script> element, either in the <head> section or at the end of the <body> section to improve page loading performance.

Moving forward, the <body> element encapsulates the main content of the web page, including text, images, links, and other multimedia elements. Within the <body> element, developers can use a variety of HTML tags and attributes to structure and format the content according to the desired layout and design. For example, headings are denoted by the <h1> to <h6> tags, with <h1> representing the highest level of heading and <h6> representing the lowest level. Paragraphs of text can be enclosed within the <p> tags, while lists can be created using the <ul>, <ol>, and <li> tags for unordered and ordered lists, respectively.

Furthermore, images can be embedded in the HTML document using the <img> tag, with the src attribute specifying the path to the image file and the alt attribute providing alternative text for screen readers and search engines. Hyperlinks, or anchor links, are created using the <a> tag, with the href attribute specifying the destination URL and the text between the opening and closing <a> tags serving as the clickable link text. Additionally, developers can use semantic HTML elements, such as <header>, <footer>, <nav>, and <article>, to provide meaningful structure and improve accessibility for assistive technologies.

As developers work on more complex web projects, they may encounter the need to include interactive elements and dynamic content in their HTML documents. This can be achieved using scripting languages like JavaScript, which allow for client-side interactivity and manipulation of the DOM (Document Object Model). To include JavaScript code in an HTML document, developers can use the <script> element with the src attribute pointing to an external JavaScript file or include the JavaScript code directly within the <script> tags. By leveraging JavaScript frameworks and libraries like React, Vue.js, or Angular, developers can build interactive web applications with rich user experiences.

In summary, understanding the anatomy of an HTML document is essential for web developers to create well-structured and accessible websites. By following the standards and best practices outlined in the HTML specification, developers can ensure compatibility across different browsers and devices and provide an optimal user experience for visitors to their web pages. With the ever-evolving landscape of web technologies, staying updated on the latest HTML features and techniques is crucial for building modern and responsive web applications.

Chapter 2: Basic Tags and Elements: Getting Started with HTML

HTML, the backbone of web development, comprises a multitude of tags that play crucial roles in structuring and formatting web content. Understanding these tags is fundamental for any web developer aiming to craft cohesive and well-organized web pages. Let's delve into the world of common HTML tags, exploring their purposes, syntax, and practical applications.

htmlCopy code

```
<!DOCTYPE html> <html lang="en"> <head>
<meta charset="UTF-8"> <meta name="viewport"
content="width=device-width, initial-scale=1.0">
<title>Document</title> </head> <body> <!--
Heading Tags --> <h1>This is a Heading Level
1</h1> <h2>This is a Heading Level 2</h2>
<h3>This is a Heading Level 3</h3> <h4>This is a
Heading Level 4</h4> <h5>This is a Heading Level
5</h5> <h6>This is a Heading Level 6</h6> <!--
Paragraph Tag --> <p>This is a paragraph.</p> <!--
Anchor Tag --> <a
href="https://example.com">Visit Example</a> <!-
- Image Tag --> <img src="image.jpg"
alt="Description of Image"> <!-- List Tags --> <ul>
```

```
<li>Item 1</li> <li>Item 2</li> </ul> <ol>
<li>Item 1</li> <li>Item 2</li> </ol> <!-- Table Tag
--> <table> <thead> <tr> <th>Header 1</th>
<th>Header 2</th> </tr> </thead> <tbody> <tr>
<td>Data 1</td> <td>Data 2</td> </tr> </tbody>
</table> <!-- Form Tag --> <form> <input
type="text" placeholder="Enter your name">
<button type="submit">Submit</button> </form>
</body> </html>
```

Heading tags **<h1>** to **<h6>** are used to define the headings of different levels, aiding in structuring the content hierarchically. These tags are essential for organizing content and improving its readability.

Paragraph tags **<p>** are employed to denote paragraphs of text, allowing developers to separate content into meaningful sections and enhance its clarity.

Anchor tags **<a>** facilitate the creation of hyperlinks, enabling users to navigate between different web pages or resources effortlessly. The **href** attribute specifies the destination URL of the hyperlink.

Image tags **<img>** are utilized to embed images within web pages, enriching visual content and providing context to users. The **src** attribute denotes the path to the image file, while the **alt** attribute offers descriptive text for accessibility purposes.

List tags **<ul>** (unordered lists) and **<ol>** (ordered lists) are employed to create lists of items, be it bullet points or numbered items, respectively. These tags aid in organizing information in a structured and easy-to-follow manner.

Table tags **<table>** are employed to construct tables, which are useful for presenting data in a tabular format. Tables consist of rows denoted by **<tr>** tags and columns specified within **<th>** (table header) and **<td>** (table data) tags.

Form tags **<form>** are utilized to create interactive forms, allowing users to input data and submit it to a server for processing. Form elements such as **<input>** fields and **<button>** controls facilitate user interaction, while attributes like **action** and **method** determine the form's behavior upon submission.

Understanding these common HTML tags lays the foundation for creating well-structured and semantically meaningful web pages. By leveraging these tags effectively, developers can craft engaging and accessible web experiences for users across various devices and platforms.

Image insertion and attributes play a pivotal role in web development, allowing developers to enhance the visual appeal and functionality of web pages. When creating web content, integrating images is essential for capturing users' attention and conveying information effectively. In HTML, the process of inserting images involves using the **<img>** tag, along with various attributes to specify important details such as the image source, alternative text, dimensions, and more.

To insert an image into an HTML document, you first need to have the image file saved in a location accessible to your website. This could be within the same directory as your HTML file or in a subdirectory. Once you have the image file ready, you can use the **<img>** tag to display it on your web page. The basic syntax for the **<img>** tag is as follows:

htmlCopy code

<img src="image.jpg" alt="Description of Image">

In this example, the **src** attribute specifies the path to the image file, while the **alt** attribute provides alternative text that describes the image. The **alt** attribute is crucial for accessibility purposes, as it provides a textual description of the image for users who may not be able to view it, such as those using screen readers.

When specifying the image source (**src**), you can use relative or absolute paths depending on the location of your image file relative to your HTML document. If the image file is in the same directory as your HTML file, you can simply provide the filename, as shown in the example above. If the image file is in a subdirectory, you would specify the path relative to the HTML file, such as **src="images/image.jpg"**.

Additionally, you can include other attributes to further customize the appearance and behavior of the image. For example, the **width** and **height** attributes allow you to specify the dimensions of the image in pixels, helping to control its size on the page. It's important to specify both the width and height attributes to prevent the browser from resizing the image, which can lead to distorted or pixelated results.

htmlCopy code

```html
<img src="image.jpg" alt="Description of Image" width="300" height="200">
```

In this example, the image will be displayed with a width of 300 pixels and a height of 200 pixels. Adjust these values accordingly based on the dimensions of your image and the layout of your web page.

You can also use additional attributes to enhance the accessibility, responsiveness, and performance of your images. The **title** attribute allows you to provide a tooltip that appears when users hover over the image, offering additional information or context. Additionally, the **loading** attribute enables lazy loading, which defers the loading of offscreen images until they are needed, improving page load times and overall performance.

htmlCopy code

```html
<img src="image.jpg" alt="Description of Image" title="Additional Information" loading="lazy">
```

Furthermore, you can use the **srcset** attribute to specify multiple image sources at different resolutions or sizes, allowing the browser to choose the most appropriate image based on the user's device and screen resolution. This is particularly useful for creating responsive designs that adapt seamlessly to various viewport sizes and device types.

htmlCopy code

```
<img srcset="image-320w.jpg 320w, image-480w.jpg 480w, image-800w.jpg 800w" sizes="(max-width: 320px) 280px, (max-width: 480px) 440px, 800px" src="image-800w.jpg" alt="Description of Image">
```

In this example, the browser will choose the appropriate image source based on the viewport width, ensuring optimal image quality and performance across different devices and screen sizes. The **sizes** attribute specifies the width of the image at different viewport widths, while the **srcset** attribute provides a list of available image sources with their respective widths.

Overall, understanding image insertion and attributes is essential for creating visually engaging and accessible web pages. By leveraging HTML's **<img>** tag and its associated attributes, developers can seamlessly integrate images into their web content while optimizing for accessibility, responsiveness, and performance. Whether you're building a simple personal website or a complex web application, mastering image insertion techniques will empower you to create compelling and user-friendly experiences for your audience.

Chapter 3: Formatting Text and Images

Text formatting tags are essential elements in HTML that enable developers to manipulate the appearance and structure of text content on web pages. These tags provide a variety of options for styling text, including making text bold, italicizing it, underlining it, and more. Understanding how to use text formatting tags effectively is crucial for creating visually appealing and well-organized web content. Let's explore some of the most commonly used text formatting tags in HTML and how they can be implemented to enhance the presentation of text.

One of the most basic text formatting tags is the **<b>** tag, which is used to make text bold. By wrapping text in **<b>** tags, you can emphasize important words or phrases within your content. Similarly, the **<i>** tag is used to italicize text, providing a visual distinction that can help convey emphasis or convey a different tone. These tags are straightforward to use and can be applied directly to the text content within your HTML document.

htmlCopy code

```
<p>This is <b>bold</b> text and <i>italic</i> text.</p>
```

In this example, the text "bold" will appear in bold font weight, while the text "italic" will appear in italicized font style. Both formatting styles are applied inline within the paragraph (**<p>**) element, allowing for easy integration with other text content.

Another commonly used text formatting tag is the **<u>** tag, which is used to underline text. While underlining text is less common in modern web design compared to bolding or italicizing, it can still be used to denote hyperlinks or highlight specific information. Like the **<b>** and **<i>** tags, the **<u>** tag is applied inline to the text content within your HTML document.

htmlCopy code

```
<p>This is <u>underlined</u> text.</p>
```

In this example, the text "underlined" will appear with a line underneath it, indicating that it is underlined. While underlining text should be used sparingly to avoid cluttering the visual appearance of your web pages, it can be effective in certain contexts, such as indicating links or emphasizing headings.

In addition to these basic text formatting tags, HTML also provides tags for superscript and subscript text, which are often used in scientific or mathematical contexts. The **<sup>** tag is used to denote superscript text, which appears above the baseline of the surrounding text, while the **<sub>** tag is used to denote subscript text, which appears below the baseline of the surrounding text.

htmlCopy code

```
<p>This is <sup>superscript</sup> and this is
<sub>subscript</sub> text.</p>
```

In this example, the text "superscript" will appear with smaller text size and positioned above the surrounding text, while the text "subscript" will appear with smaller text size and positioned below the surrounding text. These tags are useful for indicating exponentiation, chemical formulas, footnotes, and other specialized types of text formatting.

Additionally, HTML provides tags for specifying text alignment within a document or a specific text block. The **<div>** and **<span>** tags are commonly used for grouping and styling text content, while the **align** attribute can be used to specify the alignment of text within these elements.

htmlCopy code

```
<div align="center"> <p>This is centered text.</p>
</div> <div align="right"> <p>This is right-aligned
text.</p> </div>
```

In these examples, the text within the **<p>** elements will be centered and right-aligned, respectively, within the enclosing **<div>** elements. Text alignment can help improve the readability and visual organization of your web pages, particularly for longer blocks of text or content that is displayed in columns or sections.

Overall, text formatting tags in HTML provide a versatile toolkit for customizing the appearance and structure of text content on web pages. By leveraging these tags effectively, developers can create visually appealing and well-organized web content that engages users and effectively communicates information. Whether you're emphasizing key points, denoting special characters, or aligning text within a document, understanding how to use text formatting tags is essential for mastering HTML and creating professional-quality web pages.

Image insertion and attributes are fundamental aspects of web development, allowing developers to incorporate visual elements into their web pages and enhance user experience. Images play a crucial role in conveying information, evoking emotions, and capturing users' attention, making them an integral part of modern web design. When it comes to inserting images into HTML documents, the **<img>** tag is the primary element used for this purpose. This tag allows developers to specify the source of the image file, as well as various attributes that control its appearance, accessibility, and behavior. Let's delve deeper into image insertion and explore the different attributes that can be used to customize and optimize images on web pages.

The first step in inserting an image into an HTML document is to ensure that the image file is accessible and stored in a location that can be referenced by the web page. This typically involves uploading the image file to the server hosting the website or placing it in a directory within the project's file structure. Once the image file is available, developers can use the **<img>** tag to insert it into the HTML document. The most basic usage of the **<img>** tag involves specifying the **src** attribute, which indicates the path to the image file. htmlCopy code

```
<img src="image.jpg" alt="Description of Image">
```

In this example, **"image.jpg"** represents the filename of the image file, and **"Description of Image"** is the alternative text provided for the image. The alternative text is essential for accessibility purposes, as it provides a textual description of the image for users who may be unable to view it, such as those using screen readers. Including descriptive alternative text ensures that all users can access and understand the content of the web page, regardless of their abilities or browsing environment.

In addition to the **src** attribute, the **<img>** tag supports various other attributes that can be used to customize the appearance and behavior of the image. One such attribute is **alt**, which stands for alternative text and is used to provide a textual description of the image. This attribute is crucial for accessibility purposes, as it ensures that users with visual impairments or other disabilities can understand the content of the image.

htmlCopy code

```
<img src="image.jpg" alt="Description of Image">
```

Another attribute commonly used with the **<img>** tag is **width**, which specifies the width of the image in pixels. This attribute allows developers to control the size of the image displayed on the web page, ensuring that it fits within the desired layout and does not disrupt the flow of content.

htmlCopy code

```
<img src="image.jpg" alt="Description of Image" width="300">
```

Similarly, the **height** attribute can be used to specify the height of the image in pixels. By providing both the **width** and **height** attributes, developers can ensure that the image is displayed at the correct aspect ratio and dimensions, preventing distortion or stretching of the image.

htmlCopy code

```
<img src="image.jpg" alt="Description of Image" width="300" height="200">
```

In addition to these basic attributes, the **<img>** tag supports several other attributes that can be used to enhance the appearance, accessibility, and performance of images on web pages. One such attribute is **title**, which provides additional information or a tooltip that appears when users hover over the image with their mouse cursor.

htmlCopy code

```
<img src="image.jpg" alt="Description of Image" title="Additional Information">
```

The **title** attribute can be used to provide context or supplementary details about the image, such as the name of a person depicted in a photograph or the location where the image was taken. Including informative titles helps users understand the content of images and improves the overall usability of the web page.

Another attribute that can be used with the **<img>** tag is **loading**, which specifies how the browser should load the image. The **loading** attribute supports two values: **lazy** and **eager**. The **lazy** value indicates that the image should be loaded only when it becomes visible within the user's viewport, helping to improve page load times and reduce unnecessary network requests.

htmlCopy code

```
<img src="image.jpg" alt="Description of Image" loading="lazy">
```

On the other hand, the **eager** value indicates that the image should be loaded immediately, regardless of its visibility within the viewport. This can be useful for images that are located near the top of the web page or images that are essential for understanding the content of the page.

In addition to these attributes, the **<img>** tag supports other attributes such as **srcset** and **sizes**, which are used for specifying multiple image sources and controlling how images are displayed across different devices and screen sizes. These attributes are particularly useful for implementing responsive web design techniques and optimizing images for various viewing environments.

htmlCopy code

```
<img srcset="image-320w.jpg 320w, image-480w.jpg 480w, image-800w.jpg 800w" sizes="(max-width: 320px) 280px, (max-width: 480px) 440px, 800px" src="image-800w.jpg" alt="Description of Image">
```

In this example, the **srcset** attribute specifies multiple image sources with their respective widths, while the **sizes** attribute specifies the sizes of the images at different viewport widths. By using these attributes, developers can ensure that images are displayed with optimal quality and performance across a range of devices and screen resolutions.

Overall, image insertion and attributes are essential concepts in web development, enabling developers to create visually compelling and accessible web pages. By understanding how to use the **<img>** tag and its associated attributes effectively, developers can customize and optimize images to enhance the overall user experience. Whether it's providing alternative text for accessibility, specifying image dimensions for layout consistency, or implementing lazy loading for improved performance, mastering image insertion techniques is crucial for creating professional-quality web content.

Chapter 4: Creating Hyperlinks and Anchors

Understanding hyperlinks is crucial in web development as they are the primary means of navigating between web pages and accessing different resources on the internet. Hyperlinks, also known as links or anchor tags in HTML, allow users to click on text, images, or other elements to jump to another location, whether it's within the same web page, a different page on the same website, or an external website. Mastering the use of hyperlinks is essential for creating intuitive and user-friendly navigation systems, enhancing the usability and accessibility of websites. In HTML, hyperlinks are created using the **<a>** (anchor) tag, which stands for "anchor" and is followed by the **href** attribute, specifying the destination URL of the link. Let's explore the different types of hyperlinks and how they can be used to create effective navigation systems on websites.

The most basic type of hyperlink is a link to another web page, which is created by specifying the URL of the destination page in the **href** attribute of the **<a>** tag. For example, to create a link to the homepage of a website, you would use the following HTML code:

htmlCopy code

`<a href="https://example.com">Homepage</a>`

In this example, the text "Homepage" is the clickable link that users can click on to navigate to the specified URL. When users click on the link, they will be directed to the homepage of the example.com website. This type of hyperlink is commonly used for linking to other pages within the same website, as well as for linking to external websites or resources on the internet.

In addition to linking to other web pages, hyperlinks can also be used to create internal links within the same document or page. Internal links are useful for navigating to different sections or headings within a long web page, allowing users to jump directly to the content they're interested in. To create an internal link, you can use the **id** attribute to specify an anchor point within the document, and then use the **href** attribute to link to that anchor point. For example:

htmlCopy code

`<a href="#section1">Jump to Section 1</a>` ... `<h2 id="section1">Section 1</h2>` `<p>This is the content of section 1.</p>`

In this example, clicking on the link "Jump to Section 1" will scroll the page to the heading with the **id** attribute set to "section1", allowing users to quickly navigate to that section of the document. Internal links are particularly useful for long-form content such as articles, blog posts, or documentation, where users may want to jump between different sections or topics.

Another common type of hyperlink is the mailto link, which is used to create a link that opens the user's default email client and pre-populates the recipient's email address, subject line, and body content. Mailto links are useful for providing a quick and convenient way for users to contact the website owner or support team via email. To create a mailto link, you simply specify the email address in the **href** attribute, prefixed with "mailto:".

htmlCopy code

```
<a href="mailto:example@example.com">Contact Us</a>
```

In this example, clicking on the link "Contact Us" will open the user's default email client and create a new email message addressed to "example@example.com". Users can then compose and send an email directly from their email client without having to manually enter the recipient's email address.

Hyperlinks can also be used to link to files or documents, such as PDFs, images, videos, or downloadable files. To link to a file, you simply specify the path to the file in the **href** attribute of the **<a>** tag. For example, to create a link to a PDF document named "document.pdf" located in the same directory as the HTML file, you would use the following code:

htmlCopy code

```
<a href="document.pdf">Download PDF</a>
```

In this example, clicking on the link "Download PDF" will prompt the user to download the PDF document named "document.pdf" to their local device. File links are commonly used for providing downloadable resources such as ebooks, whitepapers, or product brochures, allowing users to access and save the files for offline use.

Understanding how to create and use hyperlinks effectively is essential for building intuitive and user-friendly navigation systems on websites. By leveraging the <a> tag and its attributes, developers can create links that seamlessly connect different pages, sections, and resources, enhancing the overall usability and accessibility of websites. Whether it's linking to other web pages, creating internal navigation within a document, or providing quick access to contact information or downloadable files, mastering the use of hyperlinks is a fundamental skill for web developers.

Creating anchors and linking within a page is a fundamental aspect of web development, allowing developers to create seamless navigation experiences and improve the usability of their websites. Anchors, also known as anchor links or bookmarks, enable users to jump to specific sections within a single web page without having to scroll manually. These anchors are created using the **<a>** (anchor) tag in HTML, along with the **href** attribute to specify the destination of the link. Understanding how to create anchors and link within a page is essential for organizing content effectively and enhancing the user experience. Let's explore the process of creating anchors and linking within a page, along with best practices for implementation.

To create an anchor within a web page, you first need to identify the section of content that you want to link to. This could be a heading, paragraph, image, or any other element within the HTML document. Once you've identified the target section, you can use the **id** attribute to assign a unique identifier to that section. This identifier will serve as the anchor point that the link will navigate to when clicked.

htmlCopy code

```
<h2 id="section1">Section 1</h2> <p>This is the content of section 1.</p>
```

In this example, the **<h2>** heading element has been assigned the **id** attribute with a value of "section1". This creates an anchor point at the beginning of the section of content, allowing users to jump directly to that section when clicking on a corresponding link.

Once you've created the anchor point, you can create a link that navigates to that anchor within the same web page. To do this, you use the **<a>** (anchor) tag with the **href** attribute set to the **id** value of the target section preceded by a hash symbol (**#**). For example:

htmlCopy code

<a href="#section1">Jump to Section 1</a>

In this example, the text "Jump to Section 1" is the clickable link that users can click on to navigate to the anchor point with the **id** value of "section1". When users click on the link, the browser will automatically scroll to the specified section of the web page, bringing it into view.

Anchors and links within a page are particularly useful for long-form content such as articles, tutorials, or documentation, where users may want to navigate between different sections or topics without having to scroll through the entire page. By creating anchor points at key sections of the content and linking to them within the same page, you can provide users with a more efficient and intuitive navigation experience.

In addition to linking within the same page, anchors and links can also be used to navigate between different pages within the same website. This is achieved by specifying the relative or absolute URL of the target page in the **href** attribute of the **<a>** tag. For example:

htmlCopy code

```
<a href="page2.html">Go to Page 2</a>
```

In this example, clicking on the link "Go to Page 2" will navigate the user to the page named "page2.html" within the same website. Relative URLs are commonly used for linking to pages within the same website, while absolute URLs are used for linking to pages on external websites or resources.

When creating links between different pages within a website, it's important to ensure that the target page exists and is accessible to users. You can use relative paths to link to pages within the same directory or subdirectory, or you can use absolute paths to link to pages in different directories or on different domains.

In addition to creating links using anchor tags, you can also style links using CSS to enhance their appearance and make them stand out visually. CSS provides a variety of properties and selectors for styling links, including color, text decoration, hover effects, and more. For example:

cssCopy code

```
a { color: blue; text-decoration: none; } a:hover { text-decoration: underline; }
```

In this example, the **color** property is used to set the color of links to blue, while the **text-decoration** property is used to remove the default underline decoration from links. The **:hover** pseudo-class is used to apply a different text decoration (underline) when the link is hovered over by the user.

By combining anchors, links, and CSS styling, developers can create visually appealing and functional navigation systems that improve the overall user experience of their websites. Whether it's linking within the same page, navigating between different pages, or styling links to make them more visually prominent, understanding how to create anchors and link within a page is essential for building user-friendly and intuitive websites.

Chapter 5: Lists and Tables: Organizing Content

Creating lists is a fundamental aspect of web development, allowing developers to organize and structure content in a clear and concise manner. There are three main types of lists commonly used in HTML: unordered lists, ordered lists, and definition lists. Each type of list serves a different purpose and can be customized to suit the specific requirements of the content being presented. Understanding how to create and style lists effectively is essential for creating well-structured and user-friendly web pages. Let's explore each type of list in detail and how they can be implemented using HTML.

Unordered lists, denoted by the **<ul>** tag in HTML, are used to represent a collection of items in no particular order. Each item in an unordered list is preceded by a bullet point or some other marker, indicating that the items are of equal importance and are not ranked in any specific sequence. To create an unordered list, you use the **<ul>** tag to define the list container, and then use the **<li>** (list item) tag to define each individual item within the list.

htmlCopy code

```
<ul> <li>Item 1</li> <li>Item 2</li> <li>Item
3</li> </ul>
```

In this example, we have created an unordered list with three items: "Item 1", "Item 2", and "Item 3". Each item is enclosed within an **<li>** tag, indicating that it is a list item. When rendered in the browser, each item will be displayed with a bullet point or other default marker, depending on the browser's default styling.

Ordered lists, denoted by the **<ol>** tag in HTML, are used to represent a collection of items in a specific sequence or order. Each item in an ordered list is preceded by a numerical or alphabetical marker, indicating its position or rank within the list. To create an ordered list, you use the **<ol>** tag to define the list container, and then use the **<li>** tag to define each individual item within the list.

htmlCopy code

```
<ol> <li>First Item</li> <li>Second Item</li>
<li>Third Item</li> </ol>
```

In this example, we have created an ordered list with three items: "First Item", "Second Item", and "Third Item". Each item is enclosed within an **<li>** tag, indicating that it is a list item. When rendered in the browser, each item will be displayed with a numerical or alphabetical marker, depending on the list's sequence.

Definition lists, denoted by the **<dl>** tag in HTML, are used to represent a collection of terms and their corresponding definitions or descriptions. Each term in a definition list is preceded by a **<dt>** (definition term) tag, while each definition or description is preceded by a **<dd>** (definition description) tag. To create a definition list, you use the **<dl>** tag to define the list container, and then use the **<dt>** and **<dd>** tags to define each term and its corresponding definition within the list.

htmlCopy code

```
<dl> <dt>Term 1</dt> <dd>Definition of Term 1</dd> <dt>Term 2</dt> <dd>Definition of Term 2</dd> <dt>Term 3</dt> <dd>Definition of Term 3</dd> </dl>
```

In this example, we have created a definition list with three terms and their corresponding definitions. Each term is enclosed within a **<dt>** tag, while each definition is enclosed within a **<dd>** tag. When rendered in the browser, the terms and definitions will be displayed with the appropriate formatting to indicate their relationship within the list.

Creating and styling lists in HTML is relatively straightforward, but there are several techniques and attributes that can be used to customize the appearance and behavior of lists. For example, you can use CSS (Cascading Style Sheets) to apply custom styles to list items, such as changing the bullet point or marker style, adjusting the spacing between items, or adding background colors or borders.

htmlCopy code

```
<style> ul { list-style-type: square; } ol { list-style-type: decimal; } dl { border: 1px solid #ccc; padding: 10px; } dt { font-weight: bold; } dd { margin-left: 20px; } </style>
```

In this example, we have applied custom styles to unordered lists, ordered lists, and definition lists using CSS. The **list-style-type** property is used to specify the style of the bullet point or marker for unordered lists (**square**) and ordered lists (**decimal**). We have also added a border and padding to the definition list (**dl**), and adjusted the font weight and margin for the definition terms (**dt**) and descriptions (**dd**), respectively.

By leveraging HTML and CSS, developers can create visually appealing and well-structured lists that improve the readability and usability of their web pages. Whether it's organizing content into unordered or ordered lists, or providing definitions and descriptions using definition lists, understanding how to create and style lists effectively is essential for creating professional-quality web

Designing tables is a crucial aspect of web

development, enabling developers to organize and present data in a structured and visually appealing manner. Tables are commonly used for displaying tabular data, such as financial information, product listings, schedules, and more. Understanding how to design tables effectively involves creating a basic table structure using HTML and applying various attributes to customize the appearance and behavior of the table. Let's explore the process of designing tables, including the basic structure and commonly used attributes, along with best practices for implementation.

To create a basic table structure in HTML, you use a combination of table-related tags, including **<table>**, **<tr>**, **<th>**, and **<td>**. The **<table>** tag defines the entire table container, while the **<tr>** (table row) tag defines each row within the table. Within each row, you use the **<th>** (table header) tag to define header cells, and the **<td>** (table data) tag to define data cells. Here's an example of a basic table structure:

htmlCopy code

```
<table> <tr> <th>Column 1</th> <th>Column 2</th> <th>Column 3</th> </tr> <tr> <td>Data 1</td> <td>Data 2</td> <td>Data 3</td> </tr> <tr> <td>Data 4</td> <td>Data 5</td> <td>Data 6</td> </tr> </table>
```

In this example, we have created a simple table with three columns and two rows. The first row contains table header cells (**<th>**) to define column headings, while the subsequent rows contain table data cells (**<td>**) to display data within each column. When rendered in the browser, the table will display with borders separating the cells and aligning the content within each column.

To further customize the appearance and behavior of the table, you can apply various attributes to the table and its elements. One commonly used attribute is the **border** attribute, which specifies the width of the border around the table and its cells. You can set the value of the **border** attribute to control the thickness of the border, or you can omit the attribute altogether to remove the border entirely.

htmlCopy code

```
<table border="1"> <!-- Table content goes here -->
</table>
```

In this example, we have applied a border attribute with a value of "1" to the **<table>** tag, indicating that the table should have a border with a thickness of one pixel. Adjusting the value of the **border** attribute allows you to control the thickness of the border to achieve the desired visual effect.

Another useful attribute for styling tables is the **cellpadding** attribute, which specifies the amount of space between the content of each cell and its border. By setting the value of the **cellpadding** attribute, you can control the amount of padding around the content within each cell, ensuring that the table is visually appealing and easy to read.

htmlCopy code

```
<table cellpadding="5"> <!-- Table content goes here --> </table>
```

In this example, we have applied a cellpadding attribute with a value of "5" to the **<table>** tag, indicating that each cell should have a padding of five pixels around its content. Adjusting the value of the **cellpadding** attribute allows you to control the amount of space between the content and the border of each cell, improving the readability and aesthetics of the table.

Similarly, the **cellspacing** attribute can be used to specify the amount of space between cells within the table. By setting the value of the **cellspacing** attribute, you can control the spacing between adjacent cells, ensuring that the table is visually balanced and well-organized.

htmlCopy code

```
<table cellspacing="10"> <!-- Table content goes here --> </table>
```

In this example, we have applied a cellspacing attribute with a value of "10" to the **<table>** tag, indicating that there should be a spacing of ten pixels between adjacent cells within the table. Adjusting the value of the **cellspacing** attribute allows you to control the amount of space between cells, creating a more visually appealing and readable table.

In addition to these basic attributes, there are many other attributes and CSS properties that can be applied to tables to further customize their appearance and behavior. These include attributes for controlling the alignment of content within cells (**align**, **valign**), specifying column and row widths (**width**, **height**), and formatting text and borders (**bgcolor**, **bordercolor**, **border-collapse**), among others.

By leveraging HTML attributes and CSS styling, developers can create tables that are not only visually appealing but also functional and accessible. Whether it's displaying tabular data, creating schedules or calendars, or presenting product listings, understanding how to design tables effectively is essential for creating professional-quality web pages. With the right combination of structure, attributes, and styling, tables can be a powerful tool for organizing and presenting information in a clear and intuitive manner.

Chapter 6: Forms and Input Elements: User Interaction

Building forms is a crucial aspect of web development, enabling developers to collect user input and interact with website visitors effectively. Forms are used for various purposes, such as gathering user feedback, processing orders, registering users, and more. Understanding how to structure forms and implement form controls using HTML is essential for creating interactive and user-friendly web pages. Let's explore the process of building forms, including the basic form structure and commonly used form controls, along with best practices for implementation.

To create a basic form structure in HTML, you use the **<form>** tag to define the entire form container. Within the **<form>** tag, you include various form controls, such as text fields, checkboxes, radio buttons, dropdown lists, and buttons, to collect user input. Each form control is represented by a specific HTML element, such as **<input>**, **<textarea>**, **<select>**, and **<button>**. Let's examine the basic structure of a form and how different form controls are implemented.

htmlCopy code

```
<form> <!-- Form controls go here --> </form>
```

In this example, we have defined a simple form container using the **<form>** tag. Inside the **<form>** tag, we can include various form controls to collect user input and interact with website visitors. Let's explore some of the most commonly used form controls and how they can be implemented within a form.

Text fields, represented by the **<input>** tag with a type attribute of "text", are used to collect single-line text input from users. Text fields are commonly used for collecting names, email addresses, passwords, and other types of textual information. To create a text field, you use the **<input>** tag with the type attribute set to "text".

htmlCopy code

```
<input type="text" name="username" placeholder="Enter your username">
```

In this example, we have created a text field for collecting usernames. The name attribute is used to specify the name of the input field, which is used to identify the input data when the form is submitted. The placeholder attribute is used to provide a hint or example text to users, indicating the expected input format.

Textarea elements, represented by the **<textarea>** tag, are used to collect multi-line text input from users. Textareas are commonly used for collecting longer text input, such as comments, feedback, or messages. To create a textarea element, you use the **<textarea>** tag.

htmlCopy code

```
<textarea name="message" rows="4" cols="50" placeholder="Enter your message"></textarea>
```

In this example, we have created a textarea element for collecting user messages. The name attribute is used to specify the name of the textarea field, while the rows and cols attributes are used to define the number of rows and columns of the textarea, respectively. The placeholder attribute is used to provide a hint or example text to users, indicating the expected input format.

Checkboxes, represented by the **<input>** tag with a type attribute of "checkbox", are used to collect binary (yes/no) input from users. Checkboxes allow users to select one or more options from a list of choices. To create a checkbox, you use the **<input>** tag with the type attribute set to "checkbox".

htmlCopy code

```
<input type="checkbox" name="subscribe" id="subscribe" value="1"> <label for="subscribe">Subscribe to our newsletter</label>
```

In this example, we have created a checkbox for subscribing to a newsletter. The name attribute is used to specify the name of the checkbox field, which is used to identify the input data when the form is submitted. The id attribute is used to uniquely identify the checkbox, while the value attribute is used to specify the value of the checkbox when it is checked.

Radio buttons, represented by the **<input>** tag with a type attribute of "radio", are used to collect mutually exclusive input from users. Radio buttons allow users to select one option from a list of choices. To create a radio button, you use the **<input>** tag with the type attribute set to "radio".

htmlCopy code

```html
<input type="radio" name="gender" id="male" value="male"> <label for="male">Male</label>
<input type="radio" name="gender" id="female" value="female"> <label for="female">Female</label>
```

In this example, we have created two radio buttons for selecting the gender. Both radio buttons have the same name attribute, which groups them together as part of the same radio button group. The id attribute is used to uniquely identify each radio button, while the value attribute is used to specify the value of each radio button when it is selected.

Dropdown lists, represented by the **<select>** tag with nested **<option>** tags, are used to collect single-choice input from users. Dropdown lists allow users to select one option from a list of choices. To create a dropdown list, you use the **<select>** tag with nested **<option>** tags for each option in the list.

htmlCopy code

```
<select name="country"> <option value="usa">United States</option> <option value="uk">United Kingdom</option> <option value="canada">Canada</option> </select>
```

In this example, we have created a dropdown list for selecting the user's country. Each **<option>** tag represents an option in the dropdown list, with the value attribute specifying the value of each option and the text content specifying the display text.

Form validation and submission are essential components of web development, ensuring that user input is accurate and securely transmitted to the server for processing. Form validation involves verifying the data entered by users to ensure it meets certain criteria or constraints, such as required fields, correct formatting, and valid values. This helps prevent errors and improve the accuracy of the data collected through forms. Once the data is validated, it can be submitted to the server for further processing, such as storing in a database, sending emails, or performing other actions based on the user's input. Let's explore the techniques and best practices for implementing form validation and submission in web applications.

One common approach to form validation is using client-side validation, which involves checking the data entered by users in the browser before submitting it to the server. This provides immediate feedback to users and helps prevent unnecessary server requests for invalid data. Client-side validation can be implemented using JavaScript, which allows developers to write custom validation logic to check various aspects of the form data.

```javascript
javascriptCopy code
document.getElementById("myForm").addEventListener("submit", function(event) { // Prevent the form from submitting event.preventDefault(); // Validate form fields var name = document.getElementById("name").value; var email = document.getElementById("email").value; var password = document.getElementById("password").value; if (name === "") { alert("Name is required"); return; } if (email === "") { alert("Email is required"); return; } if (password === "") { alert("Password is required"); return; } // If all fields are valid, submit the form this.submit(); });
```

In this example, we use JavaScript to listen for the form's submit event and prevent it from submitting using **event.preventDefault()**. Then, we retrieve the values of the form fields and validate them. If any field is empty, we display an alert message to the user. If all fields are valid, we submit the form using **this.submit()**.

Another approach to form validation is using HTML5 form validation attributes, which allow developers to specify validation constraints directly in the HTML markup. HTML5 introduced several new attributes, such as **required**, **pattern**, **min**, **max**, **maxlength**, and **minlength**, which can be added to form fields to enforce validation rules.

htmlCopy code

```
<form> <input type="text" id="name"
name="name" required> <input type="email"
id="email" name="email" required> <input
type="password" id="password" name="password"
minlength="8" required> <button
type="submit">Submit</button> </form>
```

In this example, we use the **required** attribute to mark the name, email, and password fields as required. We also use the **minlength** attribute to specify that the password must be at least 8 characters long. The browser will automatically enforce these validation rules and display error messages if the user tries to submit the form with invalid data.

While client-side validation provides immediate feedback to users, it's essential to perform server-side validation as well to ensure the security and integrity of the data. Server-side validation involves revalidating the form data on the server before processing it, as client-side validation can be bypassed or manipulated by users. This helps prevent malicious attacks, such as SQL injection, cross-site scripting (XSS), and other security vulnerabilities.

javascriptCopy code

```
app.post("/submit", function(req, res) { var name
= req.body.name; var email = req.body.email;
var password = req.body.password; if (!name ||
!email || !password) { res.status(400).json({
error: "All fields are required" }); return; } if
(password.length < 8) { res.status(400).json({
error: "Password must be at least 8 characters
long" }); return; } // Process the form data });
```

In this example, we use server-side validation in a Node.js application to validate the form data received from the client. We check if the name, email, and password fields are present and not empty. If any field is missing or empty, we return a 400 Bad Request response with an error message. We also check if the password is at least 8 characters long and return an error message if it's not.

Once the form data is validated both on the client and server sides, it can be submitted for further processing. Depending on the requirements of the application, the form data can be stored in a database, sent via email, integrated with third-party services, or used to perform other actions based on the user's input.

javascriptCopy code

```javascript
app.post("/submit", function(req, res) { var name
= req.body.name; var email = req.body.email;
var password = req.body.password; // Process the
form data // Save to database, send email, etc.
res.status(200).json({ success: "Form submitted
successfully" }); });
```

In this example, we process the validated form data in a Node.js application by saving it to a database, sending an email, or performing other actions based on the application's requirements. Once the form data is successfully processed, we return a 200 OK response with a success message to the client.

Chapter 7: Semantic HTML: Enhancing Accessibility and SEO

Semantic elements play a crucial role in web development, providing meaning and structure to the content of web pages. These elements are specifically designed to describe the purpose of different parts of a web page, making it easier for both developers and web browsers to understand and interpret the content. By using semantic elements appropriately, developers can improve accessibility, search engine optimization (SEO), and the overall user experience of their websites. Let's delve into the significance of semantic elements and how they are employed in modern web development.

One of the most fundamental semantic elements in HTML is the **<header>** tag, which is used to define the header or top section of a web page. This element typically contains introductory content, such as the website's logo, navigation menu, and other essential information. By wrapping these elements within the **<header>** tag, developers indicate to web browsers and assistive technologies that this section represents the header of the page.

htmlCopy code

```
<header> <h1>My Website</h1> <nav> <ul>
<li><a href="#">Home</a></li> <li><a
href="#">About</a></li> <li><a
href="#">Services</a></li> <li><a
href="#">Contact</a></li> </ul> </nav>
</header>
```

In this example, the **<header>** tag encapsulates the website's title (**<h1>**) and navigation menu (**<nav>**), clearly delineating this section as the header. By using semantic markup, developers can enhance the accessibility of their websites, as screen readers and other assistive technologies can identify and interpret the header's purpose.

Similarly, the **<footer>** tag is used to define the footer or bottom section of a web page, typically containing auxiliary information such as copyright notices, contact details, and links to additional resources. By wrapping these elements within the **<footer>** tag, developers convey to users and search engines that this section represents the footer of the page.

htmlCopy code

```
<footer> <p>&copy; 2024 My Website. All rights
reserved.</p> <p>Contact:
info@example.com</p> </footer>
```

In this example, the **<footer>** tag encapsulates copyright information and contact details, indicating that this section serves as the footer of the page.

Search engines may use semantic elements like **<footer>** to better understand the structure and content of web pages, potentially improving the website's search engine rankings.

Another essential semantic element is the **<article>** tag, which is used to define self-contained content that can be independently distributed or reused. Articles typically represent blog posts, news articles, forum posts, or other types of stand-alone content. By wrapping such content within the **<article>** tag, developers denote to web browsers and search engines that this section contains a distinct piece of content.

htmlCopy code

```
<article> <h2>How to Create a Semantic Web Page</h2> <p>In this article, we'll explore the importance of semantic markup and how to implement it in your web pages...</p> <a href="#">Read More</a> </article>
```

In this example, the **<article>** tag encapsulates an article's title, content, and a link to read more, signaling that this section represents a standalone article. By using semantic elements like **<article>**, developers can enhance the structure and clarity of their web pages, making it easier for users to navigate and understand the content.

Furthermore, the **<section>** tag is used to define thematic groups of content within a web page, helping to organize and structure the page's content. Sections typically represent distinct parts of a page, such as chapters, modules, or functional areas. By wrapping related content within **\<section\>** tags, developers convey the hierarchical structure of the page to both users and search engines.

htmlCopy code

```html
<section> <h2>About Us</h2> <p>Learn more about our company and our mission...</p> </section> <section> <h2>Our Services</h2> <ul> <li>Service 1</li> <li>Service 2</li> <li>Service 3</li> </ul> </section>
```

In this example, two **\<section\>** tags encapsulate content about the company and its services, respectively, illustrating the distinct thematic groups of content within the page. By utilizing semantic elements like **\<section\>**, developers can improve the organization and navigation of their web pages, enhancing the user experience and facilitating search engine indexing.

Additionally, the **\<nav\>** tag is used to define navigation links within a web page, such as menus or navigation bars. By wrapping navigation links within the **\<nav\>** tag, developers signify to web browsers and assistive technologies that this section contains navigation elements, facilitating easier navigation for users.

htmlCopy code

```html
<nav> <ul> <li><a href="#">Home</a></li> <li><a
href="#">About</a></li>                <li><a
href="#">Services</a></li>                <li><a
href="#">Contact</a></li> </ul> </nav>
```

In this example, the **<nav>** tag encapsulates a list of navigation links, indicating that this section represents the navigation menu of the page. By using semantic elements like **<nav>**, developers can improve the accessibility and usability of their navigation menus, ensuring a seamless browsing experience for users.

Moreover, the **<aside>** tag is used to define content that is tangentially related to the main content of a web page, such as sidebars, advertisements, or related links. By wrapping such content within the **<aside>** tag, developers denote to web browsers and search engines that this section contains supplementary or supporting information.

htmlCopy code

```html
<aside>   <h3>Related  Links</h3>   <ul>   <li><a
href="#">Link   1</a></li>   <li><a   href="#">Link
2</a></li>   <li><a href="#">Link 3</a></li>   </ul>
</aside>
```

In this example, the **<aside>** tag encapsulates a list of related links, indicating that this section provides additional information related to the main content of the page. By using semantic elements like **<aside>**, developers can improve the clarity and organization of their web pages, making it easier for users to find relevant information.

In summary, semantic elements play a vital role in web development, providing meaning and structure to the content of web pages. By using semantic markup effectively, developers can enhance accessibility, SEO, and the overall user experience of their websites. By incorporating semantic elements like **<header>**, **<footer>**, **<article>**, **<section>**, **<nav>**, and **<aside>**, developers can create well-structured and easy-to-navigate web pages that are accessible to all users, including those using assistive technologies. By adhering to semantic best practices, developers can ensure that their websites are intelligible, efficient, and user-friendly, contributing to a more inclusive and accessible web environment.

Accessibility best practices are paramount in modern web development, ensuring that digital content is inclusive and accessible to users with diverse abilities. These practices encompass a wide range of techniques and considerations aimed at making web content perceivable, operable, understandable, and robust for all users, regardless of their disabilities or assistive technologies. Implementing accessibility best practices is not only a moral imperative but also a legal requirement in many jurisdictions, as adherence to accessibility standards such as the Web Content Accessibility Guidelines (WCAG) is mandated by law for public sector websites and often recommended for private sector websites as well.

One crucial aspect of accessibility is providing alternative text for non-text content, such as images, to ensure that users who cannot see the images can understand their content and purpose. The **alt** attribute in HTML is used to provide alternative text for images, and it should be descriptive and convey the same meaning as the image. When adding images to web pages, developers should include descriptive alt text using the **alt** attribute, allowing screen readers to convey the content of the images to visually impaired users.
htmlCopy code

```
<img src="example.jpg" alt="A person using a white cane crossing the street">
```

In this example, the **alt** attribute provides a concise description of the image, allowing visually impaired users to understand its content and context. It's essential to avoid using generic phrases like "image" or "image of" as alt text, as they do not convey meaningful information about the image.

Another critical aspect of accessibility is ensuring keyboard accessibility, allowing users to navigate and interact with web content using only a keyboard or other input devices. Keyboard accessibility is particularly important for users with motor disabilities who may have difficulty using a mouse or touchpad. Developers can ensure keyboard accessibility by ensuring that all interactive elements, such as links, buttons, and form controls, are operable via keyboard navigation.

cssCopy code

```css
:focus { outline: 2px solid #007bff; }
```

In this example, the CSS **:focus** pseudo-class is used to apply a visible outline to elements when they receive focus via keyboard navigation, providing visual feedback to users and indicating the currently focused element. It's essential to ensure that the focus indicator is visible and adequately contrasts with the surrounding content to be perceivable by all users, including those with low vision.

Another important aspect of accessibility is providing semantic HTML markup, using appropriate HTML elements to convey the structure and meaning of the content. Semantic HTML elements, such as **<header>**, **<nav>**, **<main>**, **<section>**, **<article>**, **<aside>**, and **<footer>**, help screen readers and other assistive technologies understand the purpose and organization of the content, improving accessibility and usability for all users.

htmlCopy code

```html
<header> <h1>Accessibility Best Practices</h1>
</header> <nav> <ul> <li><a
href="#introduction">Introduction</a></li> <li><a
href="#guidelines">Accessibility
Guidelines</a></li> <li><a
href="#tools">Accessibility Tools</a></li> <li><a
href="#conclusion">Conclusion</a></li> </ul>
</nav> <main> <section id="introduction">
<h2>Introduction</h2> <p>...</p> </section> <!--
Additional sections --> </main> <footer>
<p>&copy; 2024 Example Company. All rights
reserved.</p> </footer>
```

In this example, semantic HTML elements like
<header>, <nav>, <main>, <section>, and <footer>
are used to structure the content of the web page.
These elements provide valuable context and
meaning to assistive technologies, helping users
navigate and understand the content more
effectively.

Ensuring color contrast is another critical aspect of
accessibility, as low-contrast text or images can be
difficult to read for users with visual impairments,
such as color blindness or low vision. The WCAG
provides guidelines for minimum color contrast
ratios to ensure that text and images are
perceivable by users with various types of color
vision deficiencies.

cssCopy code

```
body { color: #333; background-color: #fff; } h1,
h2, h3, h4, h5, h6 { color: #007bff; }
```

In this example, CSS is used to set appropriate text and background colors with sufficient contrast to meet WCAG guidelines. It's essential to test color contrast using accessibility evaluation tools or browser extensions to ensure compliance with accessibility standards.

Providing descriptive and meaningful link text is another important accessibility best practice, as it helps users understand the purpose and destination of links without relying solely on surrounding context. Instead of using generic phrases like "click here" or "read more," developers should use descriptive link text that accurately conveys the destination or action associated with the link.

htmlCopy code

```
<a                href="https://www.example.com"
title="Accessibility   Best   Practices">Read   more
about accessibility best practices</a>
```

In this example, the link text "Read more about accessibility best practices" provides clear and descriptive information about the destination of the link, improving accessibility and usability for all users.

Implementing proper form labels and input descriptions is essential for accessibility, as it helps users understand the purpose and function of form controls and provides context for completing form fields. Developers should use the **<label>** element to associate labels with form controls and provide additional descriptive text or instructions using the **<label>** element or adjacent text.

htmlCopy code

```
<label for="username">Username:</label> <input type="text" id="username" name="username" aria-describedby="username-help"> <p id="username-help">Please enter your username.</p>
```

In this example, the **<label>** element is used to associate the label "Username" with the text input field, providing context and clarity for users. Additionally, descriptive text is provided below the input field using the **<p>** element with an appropriate **id** attribute, which is referenced in the **aria-describedby** attribute of the input field to associate the descriptive text with the input field.

Ensuring proper document structure and hierarchy is essential for accessibility, as it helps users navigate and understand the content more effectively using assistive technologies. Developers should use heading elements (**<h1>** to **<h6>**) to create a logical document structure and hierarchy, with **<h1>** representing the main heading of the page and subsequent headings representing subheadings or sections.

```html
htmlCopy code
<h1>Accessibility Best Practices</h1>  <p>...</p>
<h2>Introduction</h2>                  <p>...</p>
<h2>Accessibility Guidelines</h2> <p>...</p>
```

In this example, heading elements are used to create a logical document structure and hierarchy, with **<h1>** representing the main heading of the page and **<h2>** representing subheadings for different sections of the content.

Providing alternative text for multimedia content, such as images, videos, and audio files, is essential for accessibility, as it allows users who cannot perceive the content to understand its purpose and context. Developers should use the **alt** attribute for images, **<track>** element for video captions and audio descriptions, and **<audio>** element for providing audio descriptions or transcripts for audio files.

Chapter 8: Multimedia Integration: Adding Audio and Video

Embedding audio and video content into web pages has become increasingly common, enriching user experiences and enabling multimedia presentations. With the advent of HTML5, embedding audio and video has become more straightforward and accessible, allowing developers to integrate multimedia seamlessly into their websites. Embedding audio and video content involves using HTML5 **<audio>** and **<video>** elements, which provide native support for playing audio and video files directly within web browsers without the need for third-party plugins.

The **<audio>** element is used to embed audio content into web pages, supporting various audio formats such as MP3, OGG, and WAV. To embed audio, you specify the source of the audio file using the **src** attribute and provide fallback content for browsers that do not support the **<audio>** element using nested elements or text content.

htmlCopy code

```
<audio controls> <source src="audio.mp3" type="audio/mpeg"> <source src="audio.ogg" type="audio/ogg"> Your browser does not support the audio element. </audio>
```

In this example, the **<audio>** element embeds audio content into the web page, with two **<source>** elements specifying different audio file formats (MP3 and OGG) to provide cross-browser compatibility. The **controls** attribute adds playback controls, such as play, pause, and volume, allowing users to control the audio playback.

Similarly, the **<video>** element is used to embed video content into web pages, supporting various video formats such as MP4, WebM, and OGG. Like the **<audio>** element, you specify the source of the video file using the **src** attribute and provide fallback content for unsupported browsers.

htmlCopy code

```
<video controls> <source src="video.mp4" type="video/mp4"> <source src="video.webm" type="video/webm"> Your browser does not support the video element. </video>
```

In this example, the **<video>** element embeds video content into the web page, with two **<source>** elements specifying different video file formats (MP4 and WebM) for broader browser compatibility. The **controls** attribute adds playback controls to the video player, allowing users to play, pause, rewind, and adjust the volume of the video.

Embedding audio and video content using HTML5 **<audio>** and **<video>** elements provides several advantages, including native browser support, improved performance, and better accessibility. However, it's essential to consider accessibility when embedding multimedia content to ensure that it is perceivable and operable by all users, including those with disabilities or assistive technologies.

One crucial aspect of accessibility is providing alternative text for multimedia content, such as audio and video, to ensure that users who cannot perceive the content can understand its purpose and context. For audio content, alternative text can be provided using the **<track>** element to specify captions or subtitles, allowing users with hearing impairments to follow along with the audio content. htmlCopy code

```
<video controls> <source src="video.mp4" type="video/mp4"> <track src="captions.vtt" kind="subtitles" srclang="en" label="English subtitles"> Your browser does not support the video element. </video>
```

In this example, the **<track>** element is used to specify subtitles for the video content, with the **src** attribute pointing to a WebVTT (Web Video Text Tracks) file containing the caption text. The **kind** attribute specifies the type of text track, such as subtitles, captions, descriptions, or chapters, while the **srclang** attribute specifies the language of the subtitles.

For video content, providing descriptive and meaningful alternative text can be challenging, as videos often contain complex visual and auditory information. However, developers can provide alternative text or descriptions in the surrounding text or use additional HTML elements to provide context and explanations for the video content.

htmlCopy code

```
<video controls> <source src="video.mp4" type="video/mp4"> Your browser does not support the video element. </video> <p>This video demonstrates the process of assembling a DIY bookshelf using common household tools and materials.</p>
```

In this example, a paragraph element (**<p>**) is used to provide descriptive text for the video content, explaining its purpose and context to users who cannot perceive the video. This additional text helps users understand the content of the video and its relevance to the web page.

When embedding audio and video content into web pages, developers should also consider performance optimization to ensure fast loading times and smooth playback. This can be achieved by optimizing audio and video files for the web, using appropriate codecs and compression techniques to reduce file sizes without compromising quality.

bashCopy code

```
ffmpeg -i input.mp4 -c:v libx264 -crf 23 -c:a aac -
strict experimental -b:a 128k output.mp4
```

In this example, the FFmpeg command-line tool is used to transcode a video file (**input.mp4**) using the H.264 video codec (**libx264**) and the AAC audio codec (**aac**) with a target bitrate of 128 kbps. The resulting output file (**output.mp4**) is optimized for web playback with reduced file size and improved compatibility across different devices and browsers.

Similarly, audio files can be optimized for the web using tools like FFmpeg or audio editing software to reduce file sizes and ensure compatibility with a wide range of devices and browsers. By optimizing multimedia files for the web, developers can improve loading times and user experience while ensuring accessibility for all users.

In summary, embedding audio and video content into web pages using HTML5 **<audio>** and **<video>** elements provides a powerful way to enhance user experiences and convey information effectively. By following accessibility best practices, such as providing alternative text, captions, and descriptions, developers can ensure that multimedia content is accessible to all users, including those with disabilities or assistive technologies. Additionally, performance optimization techniques help improve loading times and ensure smooth playback across different devices and browsers, further enhancing the overall user experience.

Customizing multimedia playback on web pages offers developers a way to enhance user experiences and tailor the presentation of audio and video content to match the design and functionality of their websites. Through a variety of techniques, developers can modify the appearance, behavior, and controls of multimedia players to meet specific requirements and preferences. These customization options include styling the player interface, adding custom controls, implementing responsive design, and integrating advanced features such as playlists and subtitles.

Styling the player interface is a fundamental aspect of customizing multimedia playback, allowing developers to match the appearance of the player to the overall design theme of the website. This can be achieved using CSS to customize the colors, sizes, fonts, and layout of the player elements, such as play/pause buttons, progress bars, volume controls, and fullscreen buttons.

cssCopy code

```
/* Custom styles for the video player */ .video-player { width: 100%; max-width: 800px; margin: 0 auto; } .video-player-controls { background-color: rgba(0, 0, 0, 0.7); color: #fff; } .video-
```

player-button { background-color: transparent; border: none; color: #fff; cursor: pointer; } /* Custom styles for the audio player */ .audio-player { width: 100%; max-width: 400px; margin: 0 auto; } .audio-player-controls { background-color: #f2f2f2; border: 1px solid #ccc; border-radius: 5px; }

In this example, custom CSS styles are applied to video and audio players to customize their appearance. The **.video-player** and **.audio-player** classes define the overall layout and dimensions of the players, while **.video-player-controls** and **.audio-player-controls** customize the appearance of the player controls.

Adding custom controls to multimedia players allows developers to extend the functionality of the default player interface and provide additional features or interactions for users. This can be achieved using JavaScript to manipulate the player elements and respond to user actions, such as play/pause, volume adjustment, seeking, and fullscreen mode.

htmlCopy code

```
<!-- Custom controls for the video player --> <div class="video-player-controls">        <button class="video-player-button" onclick="togglePlayPause()">Play/Pause</button> <input type="range" class="video-player-slider"
```

min="0" max="100" value="0" step="1" onchange="seekVideo()"> <button class="video-player-button" onclick="toggleMute()">Mute/Unmute</button> </div> <!-- Custom controls for the audio player --> <div class="audio-player-controls"> <button class="audio-player-button" onclick="togglePlayPause()">Play/Pause</button> <input type="range" class="audio-player-slider" min="0" max="100" value="0" step="1" onchange="adjustVolume()"> </div> <script> function togglePlayPause() { // Toggle play/pause state of the player } function seekVideo() { // Seek to the specified position in the video } function toggleMute() { // Toggle mute/unmute state of the player } function adjustVolume() { // Adjust the volume of the player } </script>

In this example, custom controls are added to the video and audio players using HTML and JavaScript. The **togglePlayPause(), seekVideo(), toggleMute(),** and **adjustVolume()** functions handle user interactions and modify the playback behavior of the players accordingly.

Implementing responsive design for multimedia players ensures that they adapt and resize appropriately to different screen sizes and devices, providing a consistent and optimized viewing experience across desktops, tablets, and smartphones. This can be achieved using CSS media queries to adjust the player dimensions, layout, and controls based on the viewport size and device characteristics.

cssCopy code

@media screen and (max-width: 600px) { /* Responsive styles for small screens */ .video-player, .audio-player { max-width: 100%; } }

In this example, a CSS media query is used to apply responsive styles to video and audio players for screens with a maximum width of 600 pixels or less. This ensures that the players resize proportionally to fit smaller screens, preventing content overflow and ensuring usability on mobile devices.

Integrating advanced features such as playlists and subtitles enhances the functionality and usability of multimedia players, providing users with more control and options for accessing and interacting with audio and video content. Playlists allow users to queue multiple media files for sequential playback, while subtitles provide textual translations or transcriptions of audio content for users with hearing impairments or language barriers.

htmlCopy code

```
<!-- Video player with playlist --> <video controls>
<source src="video1.mp4" type="video/mp4">
<source src="video2.mp4" type="video/mp4">
```

```html
</video> <!-- Audio player with subtitles --> <audio
controls>         <source         src="audio.mp3"
type="audio/mpeg">    <track   src="subtitles.vtt"
kind="subtitles"    srclang="en"    label="English
subtitles"> </audio>
```

In this example, a video player with a playlist and an audio player with subtitles are implemented using HTML5 **<video>** and **<audio>** elements. The **source** elements specify multiple media files for the playlist and the primary audio source, while the **<track>** element specifies subtitles for the audio content.

Customizing multimedia playback on web pages offers developers a wide range of options for enhancing user experiences and providing more engaging and interactive content. By styling the player interface, adding custom controls, implementing responsive design, and integrating advanced features such as playlists and subtitles, developers can create multimedia experiences that are tailored to the unique requirements and preferences of their audience.

Chapter 9: CSS Fundamentals: Styling Your HTML

CSS, or Cascading Style Sheets, is a fundamental technology in web development, providing the means to control the visual presentation of HTML and XML documents. It allows developers to define styles, such as colors, fonts, layout, and animations, to create visually appealing and user-friendly websites. Understanding CSS is essential for anyone venturing into web development, as it forms the backbone of modern web design. CSS enables developers to separate content from presentation, making it easier to maintain and update websites. This separation of concerns improves code readability and scalability, as changes to the design can be made without altering the underlying content. The syntax of CSS is relatively simple and intuitive, consisting of selectors and declaration blocks. Selectors target HTML elements to apply styles, while declaration blocks contain one or more property-value pairs defining the appearance of selected elements. For example, the following CSS rule sets the color of all **<h1>** elements to red:
cssCopy code
h1 { color: red; }
In this rule, **h1** is the selector targeting all **<h1>** elements, and **color: red;** is the declaration block

specifying the color property with a value of red. CSS supports a wide range of selectors, allowing developers to target elements based on their type, class, ID, attributes, and relationships with other elements. This flexibility enables fine-grained control over styling and layout, facilitating the creation of complex and responsive designs. For example, the following CSS rule sets the background color of all elements with the class "container" to gray:

cssCopy code

```
.container { background-color: #f0f0f0; }
```

In this rule, **.container** is the selector targeting all elements with the class "container", and **background-color: #f0f0f0;** is the declaration block setting the background color to a light gray. CSS also supports inheritance and cascading, allowing styles to be inherited from parent elements and overridden by more specific styles. This hierarchical nature of CSS enables developers to define global styles that apply to the entire document and override them with more specific styles for individual elements or sections. For example, consider the following HTML markup:

htmlCopy code

```
<!DOCTYPE html> <html> <head> <title>Sample Page</title> <style> body { font-family: Arial, sans-serif; font-size: 16px; color: #333; } .header {
```

background-color: #007bff; color: #fff; padding: 10px; } </style> </head> <body> <div class="header"> <h1>Welcome to Our Website</h1> </div> <p>This is a sample paragraph.</p> </body> </html>

In this example, the **<style>** element contains CSS rules defining styles for the body and **.header** elements. The body styles set the font family, font size, and text color for the entire document, while the **.header** styles set the background color, text color, and padding for the header section. The styles defined in the **<style>** element override any default browser styles, ensuring a consistent and visually appealing presentation across different browsers and devices.

CSS also offers powerful layout capabilities, allowing developers to control the positioning, size, and alignment of elements on a web page. Flexbox and Grid layout are two modern CSS layout models that provide flexible and efficient ways to create complex and responsive layouts. Flexbox is particularly well-suited for one-dimensional layouts, such as navigation menus and card grids, while Grid layout excels at creating two-dimensional layouts, such as magazine-style columns and image galleries. For example, consider the following CSS code using Flexbox to create a horizontal navigation menu:
cssCopy code

.nav { display: flex; justify-content: space-between; } .nav-item { margin: 0 10px; } .nav-link { text-decoration: none; color: #333; }

In this example, the **.nav** class applies Flexbox layout to the navigation menu, distributing the menu items evenly along the main axis (horizontal axis) with space between them. The **.nav-item** class sets margins around each menu item, and the **.nav-link** class styles the links within the menu.

In addition to layout, CSS enables developers to create interactive and dynamic web experiences through animations and transitions. CSS animations allow elements to move, change size, rotate, and fade in or out smoothly, adding visual interest and engagement to websites. Transitions provide a way to animate changes in CSS properties over time, such as color, opacity, and position, creating fluid and responsive user interfaces. By combining CSS animations and transitions with JavaScript, developers can create sophisticated and interactive web applications with rich multimedia experiences.

For example, consider the following CSS code using keyframe animations to create a simple animation of a bouncing ball:

cssCopy code

@keyframes bounce { 0% { transform: translateY(0); } 50% { transform: translateY(-50px); } 100% { transform: translateY(0); } } .ball {

width: 50px; height: 50px; background-color: #007bff; position: relative; animation: bounce 1s infinite; }

In this example, the **@keyframes** rule defines a set of keyframes for the **bounce** animation, specifying the vertical translation of the ball at different points in time. The **.ball** class styles the ball element with a blue background color, and the **animation** property applies the **bounce** animation to the ball element, causing it to bounce up and down indefinitely.

Overall, CSS is a powerful and versatile technology that plays a central role in modern web development. By mastering CSS, developers can create visually stunning, responsive, and interactive websites that engage users and deliver an exceptional user experience. With its rich set of features, including selectors, inheritance, cascading, layouts, animations, and transitions, CSS empowers developers to bring their design visions to life on the web.

Applying CSS styles to HTML elements is a fundamental aspect of web development, allowing developers to control the appearance and layout of web pages. By defining styles for HTML elements, developers can customize the look and feel of their websites to create visually appealing and user-friendly experiences. CSS styles can be applied to

HTML elements using various methods, including inline styles, internal stylesheets, and external stylesheets.

Inline styles are CSS styles applied directly to individual HTML elements using the **style** attribute. This method is useful for adding quick and specific styles to individual elements without affecting other elements on the page. Inline styles override any styles defined in external or internal stylesheets, making them ideal for applying temporary or one-off styles.

htmlCopy code

```
<p style="color: blue; font-size: 18px;">This is a paragraph with inline styles.</p>
```

In this example, the **style** attribute is used to apply inline styles to a **<p>** element, setting its text color to blue and font size to 18 pixels. Inline styles are convenient for quick styling changes but can become cumbersome to manage in larger projects with many elements.

Internal stylesheets are CSS styles defined within the **<style>** element in the **<head>** section of an HTML document. This method allows developers to encapsulate styles within the HTML document itself, making it easier to maintain and update styles for multiple elements. Internal stylesheets apply to all HTML elements within the document and take precedence over external stylesheets but are overridden by inline styles.

htmlCopy code

```
<!DOCTYPE html> <html lang="en"> <head>
<meta charset="UTF-8"> <meta name="viewport"
content="width=device-width, initial-scale=1.0">
<title>Internal Stylesheet Example</title> <style> p
{ color: green; font-size: 16px; } </style> </head>
<body> <p>This is a paragraph with internal
styles.</p> </body> </html>
```

In this example, the **<style>** element contains CSS styles for **<p>** elements, setting their text color to green and font size to 16 pixels. Internal stylesheets are useful for organizing styles within a single HTML document but may lead to code duplication and maintenance issues in larger projects.

External stylesheets are CSS files separate from HTML documents, linked to HTML pages using the **<link>** element. This method allows developers to define styles in separate files, making it easier to manage and reuse styles across multiple pages and projects. External stylesheets provide better separation of concerns, allowing developers to focus on HTML structure separately from CSS styling.

htmlCopy code

```
<!DOCTYPE html> <html lang="en"> <head>
<meta charset="UTF-8"> <meta name="viewport"
```

content="width=device-width, initial-scale=1.0"> <title>External Stylesheet Example</title> <link rel="stylesheet" href="styles.css"> </head> <body> <p>This is a paragraph with external styles.</p> </body> </html>

In this example, the **<link>** element links to an external CSS file named "styles.css," which contains styles for **<p>** elements. External stylesheets offer scalability and maintainability benefits, allowing developers to modularize styles and apply consistent designs across multiple pages.

CSS styles can be applied to HTML elements using various selectors, including element selectors, class selectors, ID selectors, attribute selectors, and pseudo-class selectors. Element selectors target specific HTML elements, applying styles to all instances of that element on the page. Class selectors target elements with specific class attributes, allowing developers to apply styles to groups of elements with similar characteristics.

cssCopy code

/* Element selector */ p { color: blue; } /* Class selector */ .highlight { background-color: yellow; }

In this example, the element selector sets the text color of all **<p>** elements to blue, while the class selector applies a yellow background color to elements with the "highlight" class. Class selectors are particularly useful for styling reusable components and applying consistent styles across different elements.

ID selectors target elements with specific ID attributes, providing a way to apply unique styles to individual elements on the page. ID selectors should be used sparingly, as they have higher specificity than other selectors and can lead to style conflicts and maintenance issues.

cssCopy code

```
/* ID selector */ #header { font-size: 24px; }
```

In this example, the ID selector sets the font size of the element with the "header" ID to 24 pixels. ID selectors are useful for styling elements that appear only once on a page or have unique styling requirements.

Attribute selectors target elements with specific attributes or attribute values, allowing developers to apply styles based on element attributes such as "href," "src," or "type." Attribute selectors provide a powerful way to style elements dynamically based on their attributes, enhancing the flexibility and versatility of CSS.

cssCopy code

```
/* Attribute selector */ a[href^="https://"] { color: green; }
```

In this example, the attribute selector sets the text color of anchor elements (<a>) with "href" attributes starting with "https://" to green. Attribute selectors can be used to style links, images, form elements, and other elements based on their attributes.

Pseudo-class selectors target elements based on their state or position within the document, allowing developers to apply styles to elements in specific situations, such as when they are hovered over, focused, or visited. Pseudo-class selectors enhance the interactivity and usability of web pages by providing visual feedback to users based on their actions.

cssCopy code

```
/* Pseudo-class selector */ a:hover { text-decoration: underline; }
```

In this example, the pseudo-class selector underlines anchor elements (**<a>**) when they are hovered over by the user. Pseudo-class selectors can be used to style links, form elements, and other interactive elements based on user interactions.

In summary, applying CSS styles to HTML elements is essential for creating visually appealing and user-friendly web pages. CSS styles can be applied using inline styles, internal stylesheets, or external stylesheets, each with its advantages and use cases. CSS selectors allow developers to target specific elements and apply styles based on various criteria, such as element type, class, ID, attributes, and pseudo-classes. Understanding CSS selectors and styling techniques is crucial for web developers to create effective and engaging designs that meet the needs and preferences of users.

Chapter 10: Responsive Design: Adapting to Different Devices

Understanding responsive design principles is essential for modern web development, as it allows websites to adapt and provide optimal viewing experiences across a wide range of devices and screen sizes. Responsive design ensures that websites look and function well on desktop computers, laptops, tablets, and smartphones, catering to the diverse needs and preferences of users. At its core, responsive design is about creating flexible and fluid layouts that adjust dynamically based on the characteristics of the user's device and viewport size.

The primary goal of responsive design is to provide a consistent and user-friendly experience regardless of the device used to access the website. This is achieved through a combination of flexible grids and layouts, media queries, and flexible images and media. Flexible grids use relative units like percentages or ems rather than fixed units like pixels, allowing content to scale proportionally with the viewport size. This ensures that content remains readable and accessible on devices with different screen sizes and resolutions.

cssCopy code

```css
.container { width: 90%; /* Use percentage for
flexible width */ max-width: 1200px; /* Set
maximum width for large screens */ margin: 0
auto; /* Center the container */ } .column { width:
100%; /* Use percentage for flexible width */
padding: 0 20px; /* Add padding to the columns
*/ box-sizing: border-box; /* Include padding and
border in the width */ }
```

In this CSS example, the **.container** class sets the width of the container to 90% of the viewport width, with a maximum width of 1200 pixels to prevent content from becoming too wide on large screens. The **.column** class sets the width of individual columns to 100% of their parent container, ensuring they fill the available space while accounting for padding.

Media queries are CSS rules that allow developers to apply different styles based on the characteristics of the user's device, such as screen size, resolution, and orientation. Media queries enable developers to create responsive layouts that adapt to various viewport sizes and device capabilities, providing users with an optimized experience on both desktop and mobile devices.

cssCopy code

```css
@media screen and (max-width: 768px) { .column
{ width: 100%; /* Adjust column width for smaller
```

screens */ padding: 0; /* Remove padding for smaller screens */ } }

In this example, a media query targets screens with a maximum width of 768 pixels (typically tablet screens in portrait orientation) and adjusts the width and padding of the **.column** class accordingly. This ensures that columns stack vertically and remove padding to conserve space on smaller screens.

Flexible images and media are essential components of responsive design, as they allow images, videos, and other media content to adapt to different viewport sizes without losing quality or aspect ratio. By using relative units like percentages or max-width properties, developers can ensure that images scale proportionally with the viewport size, preventing them from overflowing or becoming distorted on smaller screens.

cssCopy code

img { max-width: 100%; /* Make images responsive */ height: auto; /* Maintain aspect ratio */ }

In this CSS example, the **max-width: 100%;** property ensures that images never exceed the width of their parent container, allowing them to scale down proportionally on smaller screens while maintaining their aspect ratio. The **height: auto;** property ensures that images adjust their height accordingly to prevent distortion.

In addition to flexible grids, media queries, and flexible images, responsive design principles also include considerations for touch-friendly navigation, font scaling, and performance optimization. Touch-friendly navigation ensures that websites are easy to navigate on touch-enabled devices, with larger touch targets and responsive menus. Font scaling ensures that text remains readable and legible across different viewport sizes, with fonts scaling proportionally to maintain readability on smaller screens.

cssCopy code

```
body { font-size: 16px; /* Set base font size */ }
@media screen and (max-width: 768px) { body {
font-size: 14px; /* Adjust font size for smaller
screens */ } }
```

In this example, a media query adjusts the base font size of the **body** element for screens with a maximum width of 768 pixels, ensuring that text remains legible on smaller screens by scaling down the font size.

Performance optimization is another critical aspect of responsive design, as slow-loading websites can frustrate users and negatively impact search engine rankings. Performance optimization techniques include minimizing file sizes, reducing the number of HTTP requests, and leveraging caching and compression techniques to improve page load times.

bashCopy code

```
# Example CLI commands for performance optimization $ npm install -g gulp-cli # Install Gulp CLI globally $ npm install gulp gulp-uglify gulp-cssnano gulp-imagemin gulp-htmlmin --save-dev # Install Gulp and plugins locally $ gulp # Run Gulp tasks to minify and optimize CSS, JavaScript, images, and HTML files
```

In this example, Gulp is used as a task runner to automate performance optimization tasks such as minifying and compressing CSS, JavaScript, images, and HTML files. By running the **gulp** command, developers can streamline the optimization process and improve the performance of their responsive websites.

Overall, understanding responsive design principles is essential for creating websites that provide optimal viewing experiences across different devices and screen sizes. By implementing flexible grids, media queries, flexible images, touch-friendly navigation, font scaling, and performance optimization techniques, developers can ensure that their websites are accessible, user-friendly, and performant on desktop computers, laptops, tablets, and smartphones.

Implementing media queries is crucial for creating responsive websites that adapt to different screen sizes and devices. Media queries allow developers to apply specific CSS styles based on the characteristics of the user's device, such as screen width, height, orientation, and resolution. By using media queries, developers can create layouts that adjust dynamically to provide optimal viewing experiences across a wide range of devices, from desktop computers to smartphones and tablets.

The syntax of a media query consists of a media type, such as "screen" or "print," followed by one or more media features enclosed in parentheses. Media features can include properties like width, height, orientation, aspect ratio, and resolution, among others. Media queries can be applied inline within HTML documents using the **<style>** element or externally in CSS files linked to HTML documents using the **<link>** element.

cssCopy code

```
/* External CSS file with media queries */ @media
screen and (max-width: 768px) { /* CSS styles for
screens with a maximum width of 768px */ }
@media screen and (min-width: 768px) and
(max-width: 1024px) { /* CSS styles for screens
with a width between 768px and 1024px */ }
@media screen and (min-width: 1024px) { /* CSS
```

styles for screens with a minimum width of 1024px */ }

In this example, three media queries are used to apply different CSS styles based on the screen width. The first media query targets screens with a maximum width of 768 pixels, the second targets screens with a width between 768 pixels and 1024 pixels, and the third targets screens with a minimum width of 1024 pixels. By using these media queries, developers can create responsive layouts that adjust smoothly across different screen sizes.

Media queries can also target specific device features, such as orientation (landscape or portrait), resolution (pixel density), and aspect ratio (width-to-height ratio). This level of granularity allows developers to fine-tune the appearance and behavior of their websites based on the capabilities and characteristics of the user's device.

cssCopy code

```
/* Media query targeting devices in landscape orientation */ @media screen and (orientation: landscape) { /* CSS styles for devices in landscape orientation */ } /* Media query targeting devices with a high pixel density */ @media screen and (min-resolution: 2dppx) { /* CSS styles for devices with a high pixel density (Retina displays) */ } /* Media query targeting devices with a specific aspect
```

ratio */ @media screen and (min-aspect-ratio: 16/9) { /* CSS styles for devices with a 16:9 aspect ratio (widescreen displays) */ }

In this example, media queries are used to target devices in landscape orientation, devices with a high pixel density (such as Retina displays), and devices with a specific aspect ratio (such as widescreen displays). By applying specific styles based on these device features, developers can optimize the layout and presentation of their websites for different devices and user preferences.

Media queries can also be combined with other CSS techniques, such as flexbox and grid layout, to create complex and flexible responsive designs. Flexbox and grid layout provide powerful tools for creating responsive layouts that adapt to different screen sizes and orientations while maintaining a consistent and visually appealing design.

cssCopy code

```
/* Flexbox layout with media queries */ .container
{ display: flex; flex-wrap: wrap; } .item { flex: 1 1
200px; /* Flexible width with a minimum width of
200px */ } /* Media query for adjusting the number
of columns based on screen width */ @media
screen and (max-width: 768px) { .item { flex-
basis: 50%; /* Two columns on screens with a
maximum width of 768px */ } }
```

In this example, a flexbox layout is used to create a responsive grid of items with a flexible width that adjusts based on the screen size. A media query is then used to adjust the number of columns displayed on screens with a maximum width of 768 pixels, ensuring that the layout remains visually appealing and functional on smaller screens.

When implementing media queries, it's essential to consider the specific needs and requirements of the website and its target audience. Testing across various devices and screen sizes is crucial to ensure that the responsive design behaves as expected and provides an optimal user experience. By combining media queries with other CSS techniques and best practices, developers can create websites that are accessible, user-friendly, and visually engaging across a wide range of devices and platforms.

Chapter 11: HTML5 Features and Modern Practices

Exploring new HTML5 elements is essential for staying up-to-date with modern web development practices and leveraging the latest features and capabilities of HTML. HTML5 introduced several new semantic elements that provide better structure and meaning to web documents, making it easier for developers to create accessible and SEO-friendly websites. These new elements offer improved semantics and functionality compared to traditional HTML elements, allowing developers to build more robust and interactive web applications.

One of the most significant additions in HTML5 is the **<header>** element, which represents introductory content or a group of navigational links at the top of a document or section. The **<header>** element is commonly used to include branding logos, site navigation menus, and introductory text on web pages. By using the **<header>** element, developers can create well-structured and accessible headers that improve the overall user experience of their websites.

htmlCopy code

```
<header> <h1>Website Title</h1> <nav> <ul>
<li><a href="#">Home</a></li> <li><a
href="#">About</a></li> <li><a
```

```
href="#">Services</a></li>                    <li><a
href="#">Contact</a></li>        </ul>        </nav>
</header>
```

In this example, the **<header>** element contains the website title (**<h1>**) and a navigation menu (**<nav>**) with a list of links (**<ul>**). By encapsulating these elements within the **<header>** element, developers can create a consistent and well-organized header section for their websites.

Another essential HTML5 element is the **<nav>** element, which represents a section of navigation links that allow users to navigate the website or document. The **<nav>** element is used to define primary and secondary navigation menus, breadcrumb trails, and other navigational elements on web pages. By using the **<nav>** element, developers can improve the accessibility and usability of their websites by providing clear and consistent navigation options to users.

htmlCopy code

```
<nav>  <ul>  <li><a href="#">Home</a></li>  <li><a
href="#">About</a></li>                    <li><a
href="#">Services</a></li>                    <li><a
href="#">Contact</a></li>  </ul>  </nav>
```

In this example, the **<nav>** element contains a list of navigation links (**<ul>**) that allow users to navigate to different sections of the website. By using the **<nav>** element to encapsulate the navigation menu, developers can create semantically meaningful navigation structures that improve the accessibility and SEO of their websites.

The **<main>** element is another important addition in HTML5, which represents the main content of the document or application. The **<main>** element is used to encapsulate the primary content of a web page, such as articles, blog posts, product listings, or other significant sections. By using the **<main>** element, developers can create well-structured and accessible main content sections that improve the overall usability and readability of their websites.

htmlCopy code

```html
<main> <article> <h2>Article Title</h2>
<p>Article content goes here...</p> </article>
</main>
```

In this example, the **<main>** element contains an **<article>** element that represents a specific piece of content on the web page. By encapsulating the main content within the **<main>** element, developers can create a clear separation between primary and secondary content and improve the accessibility and SEO of their websites.

The **<section>** element is another new HTML5 element that represents a generic section of content within a document or application. The **<section>** element is used to group related content together, such as blog posts, product listings, or chapters in a book. By using the **<section>** element, developers can create well-organized and accessible sections of content that improve the overall structure and readability of their websites.

htmlCopy code

```
<section> <h2>Section Title</h2> <p>Section content goes here...</p> </section>
```

In this example, the **<section>** element contains a heading (**<h2>**) and a paragraph (**<p>**) that represent a specific section of content on the web page. By using the **<section>** element to group related content together, developers can create a clear and structured layout that enhances the user experience of their websites.

Other new HTML5 elements include **<article>**, **<aside>**, **<footer>**, **<figure>**, **<figcaption>**, **<time>**, **<mark>**, **<progress>**, **<meter>**, **<details>**, **<summary>**, **<dialog>**, and **<template>**, among others. These elements provide developers with powerful tools for creating well-structured, accessible, and interactive web applications that meet the needs and expectations of modern users.

htmlCopy code

```
<article> <h2>Article Title</h2> <p>Article content goes here...</p> </article> <aside> <h3>Related Posts</h3> <ul> <li><a href="#">Related Post 1</a></li> <li><a href="#">Related Post 2</a></li> <li><a
```

href="#">Related Post 3</a></li> </ul> </aside>
<footer> <p>© 2024 Your Website Name. All
rights reserved.</p> </footer>

In this example, the **<article>** element represents a
self-contained piece of content, the **<aside>**
element contains related content or links, and the
<footer> element contains footer information such
as copyright details. By using these new HTML5
elements, developers can create modern and well-
structured web pages that provide an enhanced
user experience and better accessibility and SEO.

Implementing modern practices such as Flexbox,
Grid, and semantic markup is crucial for creating
efficient and well-structured web layouts. These
techniques leverage the latest advancements in
web development to build responsive, accessible,
and visually appealing websites. Flexbox and Grid
are powerful layout systems that provide
developers with flexible and grid-based approaches
to organizing and aligning content, while semantic
markup enhances the structure and meaning of
HTML documents for improved accessibility and
SEO.

Flexbox, or the Flexible Box Layout, is a CSS layout
model that allows developers to design flexible and
dynamic layouts with ease. It provides a more
efficient way to distribute space and align items

within a container, regardless of their size or content. Flexbox simplifies the process of creating complex layouts, such as navigation menus, card-based designs, and flexible grids, by offering a set of flexible properties and alignment options.

cssCopy code

.container { display: flex; /* Enable flexbox layout */ justify-content: center; /* Center items horizontally */ align-items: center; /* Center items vertically */ } .item { flex: 1; /* Grow and shrink equally */ margin: 10px; /* Add spacing between items */ }

In this example, the **.container** class enables flexbox layout, while the **justify-content** and **align-items** properties center items horizontally and vertically within the container, respectively. The **.item** class uses the **flex** property to distribute space evenly among items and adds margin to create spacing between them. By using flexbox, developers can create responsive and flexible layouts that adapt to different screen sizes and devices with minimal effort.

Grid layout, on the other hand, is a two-dimensional layout system that allows developers to create complex grid-based designs with precision. It provides a powerful way to align and position elements within a grid container, using a combination of rows and columns. Grid layout is well-suited for creating intricate layouts, such as multi-column grids, card layouts, and magazine-style designs, by defining explicit grid tracks and positioning items within them.

cssCopy code

```
.container { display: grid; /* Enable grid layout */
grid-template-columns: repeat(3, 1fr); /* Three
equal-width columns */ gap: 20px; /* Add gap
between grid items */ } .item { /* Grid item styles
*/ }
```

In this example, the **.container** class enables grid layout and defines three equal-width columns using the **grid-template-columns** property. The **gap** property adds spacing between grid items, improving readability and visual appeal. By leveraging grid layout, developers can create sophisticated and visually stunning layouts that align with modern design trends and user expectations.

Semantic markup plays a crucial role in enhancing the accessibility and SEO of web documents by providing meaningful structure and context to content. Semantic HTML elements, such as **<header>**, **<nav>**, **<main>**, **<section>**, **<article>**, and **<footer>**, describe the purpose and meaning of content within a document, making it easier for assistive technologies and search engines to interpret and navigate web pages.

```html
htmlCopy code
<header> <h1>Website Title</h1> </header>
<nav> <ul> <li><a href="#">Home</a></li> <li><a
href="#">About</a></li> <li><a
href="#">Services</a></li> <li><a
href="#">Contact</a></li> </ul> </nav> <main>
<article> <h2>Article Title</h2> <p>Article
content goes here...</p> </article> </main>
<footer> <p>&copy; 2024 Your Website Name. All
rights reserved.</p> </footer>
```

In this example, semantic HTML elements such as **<header>**, **<nav>**, **<main>**, **<article>**, and **<footer>** are used to define the structure of a web document. These elements provide valuable semantic information about the purpose and role of different sections within the document, improving accessibility for users with disabilities and enhancing the overall user experience.

By implementing modern practices such as Flexbox, Grid, and semantic markup, developers can create websites that are not only visually appealing but also highly functional, accessible, and SEO-friendly. These techniques enable developers to build responsive layouts, align content more efficiently, and provide meaningful structure and context to web documents, resulting in better user experiences and improved search engine rankings.

Chapter 12: Best Practices and Next Steps in HTML Development

Continuing your HTML learning journey is essential for mastering the intricacies of web development and expanding your skills in creating dynamic and interactive web pages. As you progress in your HTML journey, you'll encounter more advanced topics and techniques that build upon the foundational knowledge you've already gained. These advanced topics encompass a wide range of concepts, from advanced HTML elements and attributes to more complex layout and styling techniques.

One area of HTML that you can explore further is the use of multimedia elements to enhance the interactivity and engagement of your web pages. HTML provides native support for embedding various types of multimedia content, including images, audio, video, and interactive graphics. By mastering the use of multimedia elements, you can create immersive and engaging user experiences that captivate your audience.

htmlCopy code

```
<!-- Embedding an image --> <img src="image.jpg"
alt="Description of the image"> <!-- Embedding
audio    -->    <audio    controls>    <source
```

src="audio.mp3" type="audio/mp3"> Your browser does not support the audio element. </audio> <!-- Embedding video --> <video controls> <source src="video.mp4" type="video/mp4"> Your browser does not support the video element. </video>

In this example, the **<img>**, **<audio>**, and **<video>** elements are used to embed an image, audio file, and video file, respectively, into a web page. By leveraging these multimedia elements, you can create rich and interactive content that enhances the overall user experience of your website.

Another area of HTML that you can explore is the use of forms to collect user input and interact with web visitors. HTML provides a range of form elements, such as text fields, checkboxes, radio buttons, dropdown menus, and submit buttons, that allow users to input data and interact with web applications. By mastering the use of forms and form elements, you can create dynamic and interactive web forms that facilitate user interaction and data submission.

htmlCopy code

```
<!-- Example form with various form elements -->
<form action="/submit-form" method="post">
<label for="name">Name:</label> <input type="text" id="name" name="name" required>
<label for="email">Email:</label> <input type="email" id="email" name="email" required>
```

```
<label for="message">Message:</label> <textarea
id="message" name="message" rows="4"
required></textarea> <input type="submit"
value="Submit"> </form>
```

In this example, a simple form is created using HTML form elements like **<input>**, **<textarea>**, and **<button>**. Each form element collects specific user input, such as name, email, and message, which can then be submitted to a server-side script for processing. By incorporating forms into your web pages, you can create interactive and data-driven experiences that engage users and facilitate communication.

As you delve deeper into HTML, you'll also encounter more advanced layout and styling techniques that allow you to create visually stunning and responsive web designs. Techniques such as CSS Grid and Flexbox provide powerful tools for creating complex layouts with precise control over element positioning and alignment.

htmlCopy code

```
<!-- Example of using CSS Grid for layout --> <div
class="grid-container"> <div class="item">Item
1</div> <div class="item">Item 2</div> <div
class="item">Item 3</div> </div> <style> .grid-
container { display: grid; grid-template-columns:
repeat(3, 1fr); gap: 10px; } .item { background-color:
#ccc; padding: 20px; text-align: center; } </style>
```

In this example, a CSS Grid layout is used to create a grid container with three grid items arranged in a row. The **grid-template-columns** property defines the number and size of columns in the grid, while the **gap** property specifies the spacing between grid items. By combining HTML with advanced CSS techniques like CSS Grid, you can create sophisticated and responsive layouts that adapt to different screen sizes and devices.

Additionally, exploring HTML5 APIs and JavaScript integration can further enhance the functionality and interactivity of your web pages. HTML5 introduces a range of APIs for handling multimedia, geolocation, offline storage, and more, allowing you to build rich and interactive web applications that rival native desktop and mobile apps. By leveraging HTML5 APIs and JavaScript, you can create dynamic and immersive user experiences that push the boundaries of web development.

htmlCopy code

```
<!-- Example of using the Geolocation API -->
<button onclick="getLocation()">Get Location</button> <p id="demo"></p> <script>
function getLocation() { if (navigator.geolocation) {
navigator.geolocation.getCurrentPosition(showPosition);
} else {
document.getElementById("demo").innerHTML =
"Geolocation is not supported by this browser."; } }
```

```
function          showPosition(position)          {
document.getElementById("demo").innerHTML    =
"Latitude:     "   +   position.coords.latitude   +
"<br>Longitude:  " + position.coords.longitude; }
</script>
```

In this example, the Geolocation API is used to retrieve the user's current location and display it on the web page. When the user clicks the "Get Location" button, the **getLocation()** function is called, which in turn calls the **getCurrentPosition()** method to retrieve the user's coordinates. The coordinates are then displayed on the web page using JavaScript.

By exploring HTML5 APIs and integrating JavaScript into your HTML documents, you can unlock a wealth of functionality and interactivity that takes your web development skills to the next level. From multimedia manipulation to real-time communication and data processing, HTML5 APIs and JavaScript provide a vast array of tools for building modern and engaging web applications.

In summary, continuing your HTML learning journey involves exploring advanced topics and techniques that build upon the foundational knowledge you've acquired. By mastering multimedia elements, forms, layout and styling techniques, HTML5 APIs, and JavaScript integration, you can create dynamic, interactive, and visually stunning web experiences that captivate users and push the boundaries of web development. With dedication, practice, and a willingness to learn, you can expand your HTML skills and become a proficient web developer capable of building sophisticated and innovative web applications.

BOOK 2
MASTERING CSS
STYLING TECHNIQUES FOR PROFESSIONAL WEB DESIGN

ROB BOTWRIGHT

Chapter 1: Understanding the Box Model

Understanding the box model is fundamental to mastering CSS layout and design, as it governs how elements are rendered and displayed on a web page. The box model conceptualizes every element on a webpage as a rectangular box consisting of content, padding, borders, and margins. Each of these components contributes to the overall size and spacing of the element, influencing its position and appearance within the document layout.

At the core of the box model is the content area, which represents the actual content of the element, such as text, images, or other media. Surrounding the content area are the padding, which provides space between the content and the element's border. Padding can be applied to all sides of the content area or specified individually for each side using CSS properties like **padding-top**, **padding-right**, **padding-bottom**, and **padding-left**.

cssCopy code

```
/* Example of applying padding to all sides */ .box { padding: 20px; } /* Example of applying padding to individual sides */ .box { padding-top: 10px; padding-right: 20px; padding-bottom: 30px; padding-left: 40px; }
```

In this example, the **.box** class has padding applied to all sides using the **padding** shorthand property, as well as individual padding values specified for each side.

Beyond the padding is the border, which surrounds the padding and content areas, providing a visible boundary for the element. Borders can be customized in terms of color, style, and width using CSS properties like **border-color**, **border-style**, and **border-width**. Similar to padding, borders can be specified for all sides of an element or individually for each side.

cssCopy code

```
/* Example of applying a border to all sides */ .box
{ border: 2px solid #000; } /* Example of applying
borders to individual sides */ .box { border-top:
1px dashed #ccc; border-right: 2px dotted #999;
border-bottom: 3px double #666; border-left: 4px
groove #333; }
```

In this example, the **.box** class has a solid black border applied to all sides using the **border** shorthand property, as well as different border styles and widths specified for each side individually.

Finally, outside the border is the margin, which creates space between the element's border and adjacent elements in the layout. Margins can be applied to all sides of an element or specified individually for each side using CSS properties like **margin-top**, **margin-right**, **margin-bottom**, and **margin-left**.

cssCopy code

/* Example of applying margin to all sides */ .box { margin: 20px; } /* Example of applying margin to individual sides */ .box { margin-top: 10px; margin-right: 20px; margin-bottom: 30px; margin-left: 40px; }

In this example, the **.box** class has margin applied to all sides using the **margin** shorthand property, as well as individual margin values specified for each side.

Understanding how the content, padding, border, and margin interact with each other is crucial for creating well-designed and visually appealing web layouts. By mastering the basics of the box model, you gain greater control over the spacing, positioning, and overall appearance of elements on your web pages.

To inspect the box model of an element in the browser, you can use the browser's developer tools. Most modern browsers come with built-in developer tools that allow you to inspect and modify the CSS properties of elements in real-time. To access the developer tools, you can typically right-click on an element on the webpage and select "Inspect" or press **Ctrl + Shift + I** (Windows/Linux) or **Cmd + Option + I** (Mac) to open the developer tools panel.

Once the developer tools panel is open, you can navigate to the "Styles" or "Computed" tab to view the computed styles of the selected element, including its dimensions, padding, border, and margin. Additionally, many developer tools provide a "Box Model" or "Layout" section that visually illustrates the box model of the selected element, making it easier to understand how the various components contribute to its overall size and layout.

By utilizing the browser's developer tools, you can gain valuable insights into the box model of your web page elements and debug any layout issues or inconsistencies effectively. Additionally, experimenting with different padding, border, and margin values using the developer tools allows you to fine-tune the appearance and spacing of your elements in real-time, speeding up the development process and ensuring pixel-perfect layouts.

In summary, the box model is a foundational concept in CSS that governs how elements are rendered and displayed on a web page. By understanding the content, padding, border, and margin components of the box model, you gain greater control over the layout and appearance of your web pages. Leveraging the browser's developer tools allows you to inspect and manipulate the box model of elements, facilitating efficient debugging and optimization of your web layouts. Mastering the basics of the box model is essential for creating well-designed and visually appealing websites that engage and delight users.

Understanding the distinctions between margins, borders, and padding is crucial for mastering CSS layout and design, as each plays a distinct role in determining the spacing and appearance of elements on a web page. Margins, borders, and padding are all CSS properties that control the spacing around an element, but they serve different purposes and are applied in different ways.
Margins are the space between an element's border and adjacent elements in the layout. They create external space around an element, pushing neighboring elements further apart. Margins can be applied to all sides of an element or specified individually for each side using CSS properties like **margin-top**, **margin-right**, **margin-bottom**, and **margin-left**.
cssCopy code
/* Example of applying margin to all sides */ .box { margin: 20px; } /* Example of applying margin to individual sides */ .box { margin-top: 10px;

margin-right: 20px; margin-bottom: 30px; margin-left: 40px; }

In this example, the **.box** class has margin applied to all sides using the **margin** shorthand property, as well as individual margin values specified for each side.

Borders are the visible boundary around an element's content and padding. They create a visual distinction between an element and its surroundings, providing a decorative or structural element to the design. Borders can be customized in terms of color, style, and width using CSS properties like **border-color**, **border-style**, and **border-width**.

cssCopy code

```
/* Example of applying a border to all sides */ .box
{ border: 2px solid #000; } /* Example of applying
borders to individual sides */ .box { border-top:
1px dashed #ccc; border-right: 2px dotted #999;
border-bottom: 3px double #666; border-left: 4px
groove #333; }
```

In this example, the **.box** class has a solid black border applied to all sides using the **border** shorthand property, as well as different border styles and widths specified for each side individually.

Padding is the space between an element's content area and its border. It creates internal space within an element, separating its content from its border. Padding can be applied to all sides of an element or specified individually for each side using CSS properties like **padding-top**, **padding-right**, **padding-bottom**, and **padding-left**.

cssCopy code

```
/* Example of applying padding to all sides */ .box
{ padding: 20px; } /* Example of applying padding
to individual sides */ .box { padding-top: 10px;
padding-right: 20px; padding-bottom: 30px;
padding-left: 40px; }
```

In this example, the **.box** class has padding applied to all sides using the **padding** shorthand property, as well as individual padding values specified for each side.

Understanding how margins, borders, and padding interact with each other is crucial for creating well-designed and visually appealing web layouts. By leveraging margins, borders, and padding effectively, you can control the spacing, appearance, and structure of elements on your web pages.

To inspect the margins, borders, and padding of an element in the browser, you can use the browser's developer tools. Most modern browsers come with built-in developer tools that allow you to inspect and modify the CSS properties of elements in real-time. To access the developer tools, you can typically right-click on an element on the webpage and select "Inspect" or press **Ctrl + Shift + I** (Windows/Linux) or **Cmd + Option + I** (Mac) to open the developer tools panel.

Once the developer tools panel is open, you can navigate to the "Styles" or "Computed" tab to view the computed styles of the selected element, including its margins, borders, and padding. Additionally, many developer tools provide a "Box Model" or "Layout" section that visually illustrates the margins, borders, and padding of the selected element, making it easier to understand how they contribute to its overall size and layout.

In summary, margins, borders, and padding are essential CSS properties that control the spacing and appearance of elements on a web page. Margins create external space around an element, borders provide a visible boundary around an element's content and padding, and padding creates internal space within an element. By understanding how margins, borders, and padding work together, you can create well-designed and visually appealing web layouts that engage and delight users. Leveraging the browser's developer tools allows you to inspect and manipulate margins, borders, and padding in real-time, facilitating efficient debugging and optimization of your web layouts. Mastering the concepts of margins, borders, and padding is essential for creating professional-quality web designs that stand out in today's competitive online landscape.

Chapter 2: Selectors and Specificity

Understanding CSS selectors is fundamental to effectively styling HTML elements on a web page. CSS selectors are patterns used to select and style HTML elements based on their element type, class, ID, attributes, and relationships with other elements in the document structure. By mastering CSS selectors, you gain precise control over which elements to target and how to apply styles to them, enabling you to create visually appealing and well-structured web designs.

One of the simplest CSS selectors is the element selector, which targets all instances of a specific HTML element type on the page. For example, to style all **<p>** elements to have a specific font size and color, you can use the following CSS rule:

cssCopy code

```
p { font-size: 16px; color: #333; }
```

In this example, the **p** selector targets all **<p>** elements and applies the specified font size and color styles to them. Element selectors are straightforward and apply styles globally to all instances of the selected HTML element type.

Another commonly used CSS selector is the class selector, which targets elements based on their class attribute. Classes are reusable identifiers that can be applied to multiple elements on a page, allowing you to style them consistently. To target elements with a specific class, you prepend a period (.) followed by the class name to the selector. For example:

cssCopy code

.button { background-color: #007bff; color: #fff; padding: 10px 20px; border-radius: 5px; }

In this example, the **.button** selector targets all elements with the **button** class and applies the specified styles to them. Class selectors are versatile and enable you to apply styles to specific groups of elements across your web page.

In addition to class selectors, CSS also supports ID selectors, which target elements based on their unique ID attribute. IDs are unique identifiers assigned to individual elements on a page, and each ID should be unique within the document. To target elements with a specific ID, you prepend a hash (#) followed by the ID name to the selector. For example:

cssCopy code

#header { background-color: #333; color: #fff; padding: 20px; }

In this example, the **#header** selector targets the element with the **header** ID and applies the specified styles to it. ID selectors are useful for styling individual elements that have unique characteristics or serve as key components of your web page layout.

In addition to element, class, and ID selectors, CSS also provides attribute selectors, which target elements based on their HTML attributes. Attribute selectors allow you to target elements based on specific attribute values or the presence of certain attributes. For example:

cssCopy code

input[type="text"] { width: 200px; padding: 5px; border: 1px solid #ccc; }

In this example, the **input[type="text"]** selector targets all **<input>** elements with a **type** attribute set to **"text"** and applies the specified width, padding, and border styles to them. Attribute selectors provide a flexible way to target elements based on their attributes, allowing for more precise styling control.

Furthermore, CSS supports combinators and pseudo-classes, which allow you to target elements based on their relationships with other elements or their state. Combinators include the descendant selector ( ), child selector (>), adjacent sibling selector (+), and general sibling selector (~), which enable you to target elements based on their hierarchical relationships in the document structure. Pseudo-classes, such as **:hover**, **:focus**, and **:first-child**, allow you to target elements based on their state or position within the document.

cssCopy code

```
/* Example of using the descendant selector */
.container li { font-weight: bold; } /* Example of
using the :hover pseudo-class */ .button:hover {
background-color: #0056b3; }
```

In these examples, the descendant selector targets all **<li>** elements that are descendants of an element with the class **container**, while the **:hover** pseudo-class targets all elements with the class **button** when they are in a hovered state. Combinators and pseudo-classes provide powerful ways to target elements based on their relationships and user interactions, allowing for dynamic and interactive styling effects.

Understanding CSS selectors is essential for creating well-structured and maintainable CSS code. By mastering CSS selectors, you gain precise control over styling HTML elements and can create visually appealing and responsive web designs. Leveraging the various types of selectors, including element, class, ID, attribute, combinator, and pseudo-class selectors, allows you to target elements effectively and apply styles based on specific criteria.

To test and debug CSS selectors, you can use browser developer tools, such as the Elements panel in Google Chrome or the Inspector tool in

Mozilla Firefox. These tools allow you to inspect the HTML structure of a web page and test CSS selectors by applying styles in real-time. Additionally, online resources and tutorials can provide further guidance and examples for mastering CSS selectors and effectively styling your web pages.

In summary, understanding CSS selectors is essential for creating well-designed and maintainable web pages. By mastering the various types of selectors and their applications, you gain greater control over styling HTML elements and can create visually appealing and responsive web designs. With practice and experimentation, you can leverage CSS selectors to achieve the desired styling effects and enhance the user experience of your web pages.

Understanding specificity in CSS is crucial for efficiently managing styles and resolving conflicts in your stylesheets. Specificity determines which CSS rules take precedence when multiple rules target the same element. By grasping the intricacies of specificity, you can write cleaner, more maintainable CSS code and avoid unexpected styling issues.

Specificity is often represented as a four-part value, known as specificity weight, which is calculated based on the types of selectors used in a CSS rule.

Inline styles have the highest specificity weight, followed by IDs, classes, and elements. To calculate specificity weight, each type of selector is assigned a numerical value, with higher values indicating greater specificity. For example, an inline style has a specificity weight of 1000, while a class selector has a specificity weight of 10.

cssCopy code

```
/* Example of inline style */ <div style="color: red;">Inline Style</div> /* Example of ID selector */ #header { color: blue; } /* Example of class selector */ .button { color: green; } /* Example of element selector */ p { color: orange; }
```

In this example, the inline style applied directly to the **<div>** element has the highest specificity weight and will override any conflicting styles applied using other selectors. Similarly, the ID selector has a higher specificity weight than the class selector and will take precedence over it. Element selectors have the lowest specificity weight and are overridden by both IDs and classes.

Understanding specificity weight is essential for resolving styling conflicts and determining which styles will be applied to a particular element. When multiple CSS rules target the same element with conflicting styles, the browser calculates the specificity weight of each rule and applies the style with the highest specificity weight. For example, if an element has both an inline style and a class selector applied to it, the inline style will take precedence due to its higher specificity weight.

cssCopy code

```
/* Example of conflicting styles */ <div
style="color:    red;"    class="button">Inline
Style</div>
```

In this example, the inline style applied directly to the **<div>** element will override the color specified by the **.button** class selector, as inline styles have a higher specificity weight than class selectors.

To manage specificity in your CSS code and avoid styling conflicts, it's essential to write selectors that target elements with the appropriate level of specificity. Instead of relying solely on IDs or inline styles, consider using classes and descendant selectors to apply styles more selectively and maintainable. Additionally, avoid using overly specific selectors that target elements too narrowly, as this can lead to increased specificity weight and make your CSS code harder to maintain.

cssCopy code

```
/* Example of using classes and descendant
selectors */ .container .button { background-
color: #007bff; color: #fff; padding: 10px 20px;
border-radius: 5px; }
```

In this example, the **.button** class selector is nested within the **.container** class selector, providing greater specificity while still maintaining flexibility and reusability. By using classes and descendant selectors effectively, you can write CSS code that is more modular and easier to maintain, reducing the likelihood of styling conflicts and improving the overall consistency of your web design.

When encountering styling conflicts in your CSS code, you can use browser developer tools to inspect the applied styles and determine which rules are overriding others. Most modern browsers come with built-in developer tools that allow you to inspect and modify the CSS properties of elements in real-time. To access the developer tools, you can typically right-click on an element on the webpage and select "Inspect" or press **Ctrl + Shift + I** (Windows/Linux) or **Cmd + Option + I** (Mac) to open the developer tools panel.

Once the developer tools panel is open, you can navigate to the "Styles" or "Computed" tab to view the applied styles for the selected element, including their specificity weight. Additionally, many developer tools provide a "Specificity" section that displays the specificity weight of each CSS rule, making it easier to identify and resolve styling conflicts.

In summary, understanding specificity In CSS is essential for effectively managing styles and resolving conflicts in your stylesheets. By grasping the concept of specificity weight and writing selectors with the appropriate level of specificity, you can create cleaner, more maintainable CSS code and avoid unexpected styling issues in your web design. Leveraging browser developer tools allows you to inspect and debug styling conflicts, helping you to create consistent and visually appealing web designs.

Chapter 3: Cascading and Inheritance

Understanding how CSS cascades is essential for effectively styling web pages and managing stylesheets. The cascade refers to the process by which browsers determine which CSS rules apply to each element on a webpage when there are conflicting styles. CSS rules cascade based on specificity, origin, and order of declaration, allowing developers to create flexible and maintainable stylesheets that can be easily modified and extended.

The cascade operates on the principle of specificity, which determines the precedence of CSS rules when multiple rules target the same element. Specificity is calculated based on the types of selectors used in a CSS rule, with higher specificity values taking precedence over lower ones. Inline styles have the highest specificity, followed by IDs, classes, and element selectors.

To view the cascade in action, you can use browser developer tools to inspect the applied styles for an element. Most modern browsers come with built-in developer tools that allow you to inspect and modify CSS properties in real-time. To access the developer tools, you can typically right-click on an element on the webpage and select "Inspect" or press **Ctrl + Shift + I** (Windows/Linux) or **Cmd + Option + I** (Mac) to open the developer tools panel. Once the developer tools panel is open, you can navigate to the "Styles" or "Computed" tab to view the applied styles for the selected element. The browser displays the cascade order of the CSS rules, along with their specificity values, making it easier to understand which rules are taking precedence and why.

In addition to specificity, the cascade also considers the origin of CSS rules when determining precedence. CSS rules can originate from various sources, including author stylesheets, user stylesheets, and browser defaults. Author stylesheets contain the CSS rules provided by the web developer, while user stylesheets allow users to override or modify styles according to their preferences. Browser defaults serve as the baseline styles applied by the browser to HTML elements when no other styles are specified.

To override browser defaults or user stylesheets, developers can use the **!important** declaration in their CSS rules. The **!important** declaration gives a CSS rule higher precedence, ensuring that it overrides any conflicting styles, regardless of specificity. However, the use of **!important** should be avoided whenever possible, as it can lead to specificity wars and make stylesheets harder to maintain.

cssCopy code

```css
/* Example of using !important */ .button { color: red !important; }
```

In this example, the color of elements with the class **.button** is set to red with the **!important** declaration, ensuring that it overrides any other conflicting styles, regardless of specificity.

Understanding the order of declaration is also crucial in the cascade process. When multiple CSS rules target the same element with conflicting styles, the browser applies the style declared last. This means that CSS rules declared later in the stylesheet take precedence over earlier ones, regardless of specificity.

cssCopy code

```css
/* Example of order of declaration */ .button { color: blue; } .button { color: green; }
```

In this example, the color of elements with the class **.button** will be green, as the second declaration overrides the first one due to its position in the stylesheet.

To manage the cascade effectively and avoid styling conflicts, developers should follow best practices such as organizing CSS rules logically, using meaningful class names, and avoiding excessive use of **!important**. By writing clean and maintainable CSS code, developers can ensure that their stylesheets are easy to understand, modify, and extend.

In summary, understanding how CSS cascades is essential for creating well-structured and maintainable stylesheets. By grasping the concepts of specificity, origin, and order of declaration, developers can create flexible and robust stylesheets that effectively style web pages and adapt to changing requirements. Leveraging browser developer tools allows developers to inspect and debug the cascade process, helping them to resolve styling conflicts and create consistent and visually appealing web designs.

Inheritance in CSS plays a crucial role in propagating styles from parent elements to their children, simplifying the process of styling and maintaining consistency across web pages. When an element inherits a style property from its parent, it adopts the computed value of that property unless explicitly overridden. Understanding how inheritance works allows developers to write cleaner and more efficient CSS code, reducing redundancy and making stylesheets easier to maintain.

CSS properties fall into two categories concerning inheritance: inherited properties and non-inherited properties. Inherited properties are those that are passed down from parent to child elements in the

HTML document tree, while non-inherited properties are not. Properties such as font-family, font-size, color, and text-align are examples of inherited properties, meaning that child elements inherit these styles from their parent elements by default.

cssCopy code

/* Example of inherited properties */ .parent { font-family: Arial, sans-serif; color: #333; } .child { /* Inherits font-family and color from .parent */ }

In this example, the **.child** element inherits the **font-family** and **color** styles from its parent **.parent** element, resulting in consistent typography and color throughout the webpage.

However, not all CSS properties are inherited by default. Properties such as margin, padding, border, width, height, and background-color are non-inherited properties, meaning that child elements do not inherit these styles from their parent elements. Instead, child elements retain their default values for these properties unless explicitly defined.

cssCopy code

/* Example of non-inherited properties */ .parent { padding: 20px; background-color: #f0f0f0; } .child { /* Does not inherit padding or background-color from .parent */ }

In this example, the **.child** element does not inherit the **padding** or **background-color** styles from its parent **.parent** element, maintaining its default appearance for these properties.

To override inherited styles or apply additional styles to child elements, developers can use descendant selectors or target child elements directly in their CSS rules.

cssCopy code

```css
/* Example of overriding inherited styles */ .parent { font-family: Arial, sans-serif; color: #333; } .child { font-family: Helvetica, sans-serif; /* Overrides font-family inherited from .parent */ }
```

In this example, the **.child** element overrides the **font-family** style inherited from its parent **.parent** element, applying a different font family to itself while retaining the inherited **color** style.

Understanding the specificity of CSS rules is essential when working with inherited styles, as more specific selectors take precedence over less specific ones. If multiple CSS rules target the same element with conflicting styles, the browser applies the most specific rule based on the selector's specificity. By understanding specificity, developers can control the inheritance of styles and ensure that their desired styles are applied consistently across the webpage.

cssCopy code
/* Example of specificity */ .parent .child { color: blue; /* More specific selector */ } .child { color: red; /* Less specific selector */ }

In this example, the **.parent .child** selector is more specific than the **.child** selector, so the color specified in the former rule (**blue**) takes precedence over the color specified in the latter rule (**red**) when applied to the **.child** element.

While inheritance simplifies the process of styling elements in CSS, it is essential to use it judiciously and understand its limitations. Overreliance on inheritance can lead to unintended styling effects and make stylesheets harder to maintain. Therefore, developers should strike a balance between inheritance and explicit styling, using inheritance for styles that are shared among multiple elements and applying explicit styles for unique or specific styling requirements.

In summary, inheritance in CSS is a powerful mechanism for propagating styles from parent to child elements, reducing redundancy and maintaining consistency across web pages. By understanding how inheritance works and leveraging it effectively in their stylesheets, developers can create cleaner, more maintainable CSS code that is easier to manage and extend. However, it is essential to use inheritance judiciously and understand its limitations to avoid unintended styling effects and maintain control over the appearance of web pages.

Chapter 4: Working with Typography

Typography is a fundamental aspect of web design that significantly influences the readability, usability, and aesthetic appeal of a website. Understanding typography fundamentals is essential for web developers and designers to effectively communicate content and create engaging user experiences. Typography encompasses various elements, including font selection, font size, line spacing, alignment, and typography hierarchy, all of which play a crucial role in shaping the visual presentation of text on a webpage.

The choice of font is one of the most critical decisions in typography, as it sets the tone and personality of the content. Web designers can choose from a wide range of web-safe fonts or utilize web font services such as Google Fonts or Adobe Fonts to access a broader selection of typefaces. When selecting a font, it is essential to consider factors such as readability, compatibility across devices and browsers, and alignment with the website's branding and design aesthetic.

cssCopy code

```
/* Example of using Google Fonts */ <link
href="https://fonts.googleapis.com/css2?family=Ro
```

boto:wght@400;700&display=swap"
rel="stylesheet">

In this example, the Roboto font family is imported from Google Fonts and made available for use in the webpage's CSS styles.

Font size plays a crucial role in determining the readability and visual hierarchy of text content on a webpage. It is essential to strike a balance between font size and line length to ensure optimal readability across different screen sizes and devices. Typically, body text should have a font size between 16px and 20px, while headings and subheadings can vary in size to convey importance and hierarchy.

cssCopy code

```
/* Example of setting font size */ body { font-size:
16px; } h1 { font-size: 24px; } h2 { font-size:
20px; }
```

In this example, the font size for the body text is set to 16 pixels, while the font sizes for the **h1** and **h2** headings are set to 24 pixels and 20 pixels, respectively.

Line spacing, also known as leading, refers to the vertical space between lines of text. Adequate line spacing is essential for improving readability and preventing text from appearing cramped or overcrowded. The ideal line spacing varies depending on factors such as font size, line length, and typeface, but a general rule of thumb is to set the line height to around 1.5 times the font size.

cssCopy code

```
/* Example of setting line height */ p { line-height: 1.5; }
```

In this example, the line height for paragraphs is set to 1.5 times the font size, providing sufficient spacing between lines of text for improved readability.

Alignment refers to the horizontal positioning of text within its containing element. Common text alignment options include left-aligned, center-aligned, right-aligned, and justified. The choice of alignment depends on the design goals and content structure of the webpage. Left alignment is typically used for body text, while headings and other text elements may use centered or justified alignment for visual emphasis or balance.

cssCopy code

```
/* Example of setting text alignment */ p { text-align: left; } h1 { text-align: center; } h2 { text-align: right; }
```

In this example, paragraphs are left-aligned, **h1** headings are center-aligned, and **h2** headings are right-aligned.

Typography hierarchy involves establishing a visual hierarchy within text content to guide users through the information hierarchy of a webpage. Headings, subheadings, and body text are styled differently to convey their relative importance and help users navigate the content effectively. Headings are typically styled with larger font sizes, bolder weights, or different typefaces to distinguish them from body text and highlight their significance.

cssCopy code

```
/* Example of typography hierarchy */ h1 { font-size: 24px; font-weight: bold; } h2 { font-size: 20px; font-weight: bold; } p { font-size: 16px; }
```

In this example, **h1** headings are styled with a larger font size and bold weight compared to **h2** headings and paragraphs, emphasizing their importance in the typography hierarchy.

In summary, typography fundamentals encompass various elements, including font selection, font size, line spacing, alignment, and typography hierarchy, all of which contribute to the readability, usability, and visual appeal of a website. By understanding and applying these principles effectively, web developers and designers can create engaging and accessible user experiences that effectively communicate content and enhance the overall quality of a webpage.

Customizing fonts and text styles is a crucial aspect of web design that allows developers to enhance the visual appeal and readability of text content on a webpage. By leveraging CSS properties and techniques, developers can modify various aspects of typography, including font family, font size, font weight, line height, letter spacing, and text decoration, to create unique and engaging text styles that align with the website's branding and design aesthetic.

The first step in customizing fonts and text styles is selecting an appropriate font family that reflects the tone and personality of the website. Web designers can choose from a wide range of web-safe fonts or access additional fonts from web font services such as Google Fonts or Adobe Fonts. To integrate custom fonts into a webpage, developers can import the font files using **@font-face** rule in their CSS stylesheet.

cssCopy code

```
/* Example of importing custom font using @font-face */ @font-face { font-family: 'CustomFont'; src: url('custom-font.woff2') format('woff2'), url('custom-font.woff') format('woff'); }
```

In this example, the **@font-face** rule imports the custom font files (**custom-font.woff2** and **custom-font.woff**) and makes them available for use with the **CustomFont** font family.

Once the custom font is imported, developers can apply it to specific elements on the webpage using the **font-family** property in CSS. Additionally, developers can specify fallback fonts to ensure compatibility across different devices and browsers.

cssCopy code

```
/* Example of applying custom font to elements */
body { font-family: 'CustomFont', sans-serif; }
```

In this example, the custom font **'CustomFont'** is applied to the body element, with a fallback to the generic sans-serif font family for compatibility.

After selecting a font family, developers can further customize text styles by adjusting properties such as font size, font weight, line height, letter spacing, and text decoration. These properties allow developers to fine-tune the appearance of text content and improve its readability and visual appeal.

cssCopy code

```
/* Example of customizing text styles */
h1 { font-size: 32px; font-weight: bold; line-height: 1.5; letter-spacing: 0.5px; text-decoration: underline; }
```

In this example, the **h1** heading is customized with a larger font size (**32px**), bold font weight, increased line height (**1.5** times the font size), additional letter spacing (**0.5px**), and an underline text decoration.

Furthermore, developers can use CSS pseudo-elements such as **::before** and **::after** to add decorative elements or text effects to specific text content. These pseudo-elements allow developers to enhance the visual presentation of text without modifying the HTML markup.

cssCopy code

```
/* Example of using CSS pseudo-elements for text effects */ h2::before { content: '>'; margin-right: 5px; color: #ff0000; }
```

In this example, the **::before** pseudo-element is used to prepend a greater-than symbol (**>**) before each **h2** heading, with additional styling applied to the symbol.

In addition to modifying individual text elements, developers can create reusable text styles or text utility classes in their CSS stylesheet to apply consistent text styles throughout the webpage. This approach simplifies maintenance and ensures consistency in text styling across different sections of the website.

cssCopy code

```
/* Example of text utility classes */ .text-uppercase { text-transform: uppercase; } .text-muted { color: #999; }
```

In this example, the **.text-uppercase** class applies uppercase text transformation to text content, while the **.text-muted** class sets the text color to a muted gray (**#999**).

In summary, customizing fonts and text styles is a powerful technique in web design that allows developers to enhance the visual appeal and readability of text content on a webpage. By leveraging CSS properties, pseudo-elements, and utility classes, developers can create unique and engaging text styles that align with the website's branding and design aesthetic. Understanding how to select fonts, adjust text styles, and create reusable text utilities is essential for creating visually appealing and accessible web designs that effectively communicate content to users.

Chapter 5: Styling Links and Navigation

Link styling techniques play a crucial role in web design, allowing developers to enhance the visual appearance and usability of hyperlinks on a webpage. Hyperlinks are essential for navigation and content discovery, and styling them effectively can improve user experience and engagement. CSS provides various properties and techniques for customizing link styles, including color, text decoration, hover effects, visited link styles, and link states, enabling developers to create visually appealing and user-friendly link designs that complement the overall design aesthetic of the website.

The first step in styling links is defining the default link styles using CSS. Developers can use the **a** selector to target all anchor elements and apply styles such as color, text decoration, and font weight to create a consistent visual appearance for links throughout the webpage.

cssCopy code

```
/* Example of styling default links */ a { color:
#007bff; /* Blue color */ text-decoration: none; /*
Remove underline */ font-weight: bold; }
```

In this example, the default link color is set to blue (**#007bff**), the underline text decoration is removed, and the font weight is set to bold.

To differentiate between visited and unvisited links, developers can use the **:visited** pseudo-class to target visited links and apply different styles to them. By changing the color or text decoration of visited links, developers can provide visual feedback to users about their browsing history and improve navigation.

cssCopy code

```
/* Example of styling visited links */ a:visited {
color: #purple; /* Purple color for visited links */
text-decoration: underline; /* Underline visited
links */ }
```

In this example, visited links are styled with a purple color and underlined text decoration.

Hover effects are another essential aspect of link styling, allowing developers to create interactive and engaging user experiences. By using the **:hover** pseudo-class, developers can apply styles to links when users hover their mouse cursor over them, providing visual feedback and enhancing interactivity.

cssCopy code

```
/* Example of styling hover effects for links */
a:hover { color: #ff6600; /* Orange color on hover
```

/ text-decoration: underline; / Underline on hover */ }

In this example, links change color to orange and become underlined when users hover over them.

In addition to hover effects, developers can use the **:active** pseudo-class to style links when they are clicked or activated. By providing visual feedback during the click interaction, developers can improve the perceived responsiveness of the website and enhance the user experience.

cssCopy code

```
/* Example of styling active links */ a:active {
color: #cc0000; /* Red color when link is active */
}
```

In this example, links change color to red when clicked or activated.

Furthermore, developers can customize link styles based on their state within specific elements or contexts using descendant selectors or contextual selectors. By targeting links within specific containers or sections of the webpage, developers can create unique link styles that align with the design requirements of each section.

cssCopy code

```
/* Example of styling links within a navigation menu */ .nav a { color: #ffffff; /* White color for links in navigation menu */ text-decoration: none; /* Remove underline */ } /* Example of styling links
```

within a footer */ .footer a { color: #999999; /* Gray color for links in footer */ text-decoration: none; /* Remove underline */ }

In these examples, links within the navigation menu are styled with a white color, while links within the footer are styled with a gray color, each with its unique text decoration.

In summary, link styling techniques allow developers to customize the appearance and behavior of hyperlinks on a webpage, enhancing usability and visual appeal. By leveraging CSS properties and pseudo-classes, developers can create visually appealing link designs that provide clear navigation cues and improve user engagement. Understanding how to style default links, visited links, hover effects, and active links enables developers to create cohesive and user-friendly link designs that complement the overall design aesthetic of the website.

Creating responsive navigation menus is a critical aspect of web development, especially in the era of mobile-first design and varying screen sizes. With the proliferation of smartphones and tablets, ensuring that navigation menus adapt seamlessly to different devices and viewport sizes is essential for providing users with an optimal browsing experience. CSS and JavaScript offer various techniques for creating responsive navigation menus that adjust their layout and behavior based on the available screen space, enabling developers to design navigation systems that are accessible and user-friendly across desktop and mobile devices.

One common approach to creating responsive navigation menus is using CSS media queries to adjust the layout and styling of the menu based on the viewport width. Media queries allow developers to apply different styles to elements based on specific conditions, such as screen size, resolution, or device orientation. By defining breakpoints at which the layout of the navigation menu should change, developers can ensure that the menu remains usable and visually appealing across different devices.

cssCopy code

```
/* Example of using CSS media queries for responsive navigation */ @media screen and (max-width: 768px) { .nav { flex-direction: column; /* Stack items vertically */ } .nav-item { width: 100%; /* Full width for each item */ } .nav-link { text-align: center; /* Center-align text */ } }
```

In this example, the navigation menu layout is adjusted using a media query with a maximum width of **768px**, commonly used for targeting smaller devices such as tablets and smartphones. The menu items are stacked vertically (**flex-**

direction: column), each item spans the full width of the container (**width: 100%**), and the text is center-aligned (**text-align: center**).

Another popular technique for creating responsive navigation menus is the "hamburger" menu, also known as the mobile menu or toggle menu. This menu design involves collapsing the navigation links into a single icon or button (often represented by three horizontal lines resembling a hamburger) on smaller screens. When users click or tap the icon, the menu expands or slides out, revealing the navigation links. This approach conserves space and simplifies navigation on mobile devices with limited screen real estate.

htmlCopy code

```
<!-- Example of implementing a hamburger menu --> <nav class="nav"> <button class="menu-toggle" onclick="toggleMenu()"> <span class="menu-icon"></span> </button> <ul class="nav-list" id="navList"> <li class="nav-item"><a class="nav-link" href="#">Home</a></li> <li class="nav-item"><a class="nav-link" href="#">About</a></li> <li class="nav-item"><a class="nav-link" href="#">Services</a></li> <li class="nav-item"><a class="nav-link" href="#">Contact</a></li> </ul> </nav> <script> function toggleMenu() { var navList = document.getElementById('navList'); navList.classList.toggle('active'); } </script>
```

In this example, a button with the class **menu-toggle** is used to toggle the visibility of the navigation menu. Clicking or tapping the button triggers the **toggleMenu()** JavaScript function, which adds or removes the **active** class from the **nav-list** element, controlling its visibility.

Additionally, developers can enhance the usability of responsive navigation menus by incorporating touch-friendly gestures and animations. For example, swiping horizontally to navigate between menu items or smoothly transitioning the menu open and close animations can improve the user experience on touchscreen devices.

cssCopy code

```css
/* Example of CSS animation for responsive navigation */ .nav-list { transition: max-height 0.3s ease-out; /* Smooth animation */ } .nav-list.active { max-height: 200px; /* Expand height */ }
```

In this example, the **transition** property is used to create a smooth animation when expanding or collapsing the navigation menu (**max-height** property). The **ease-out** timing function ensures that the animation starts quickly and slows down gradually, providing a natural feel to the transition.

In summary, creating responsive navigation menus is essential for ensuring that websites are accessible and user-friendly across a wide range of devices and screen sizes. By using techniques such as CSS media queries, hamburger menus, touch-friendly gestures, and animations, developers can design navigation systems that adapt seamlessly to different devices and provide users with an intuitive and enjoyable browsing experience. Understanding how to implement responsive navigation menus effectively is crucial for modern web development and contributes to the overall success of a website in today's mobile-driven world.

Chapter 6: Layouts with Flexbox

Flexbox, short for Flexible Box Layout, is a powerful CSS layout model that provides developers with a comprehensive set of tools for creating flexible and efficient layouts in web applications. With Flexbox, developers can easily control the alignment, distribution, and order of elements within a container, enabling them to create complex layouts with minimal effort and code. This chapter explores the essential concepts of Flexbox and demonstrates how to leverage its features to design responsive and dynamic layouts that adapt to different screen sizes and device orientations.

At the core of Flexbox is the concept of a flex container, which is created by applying the **display: flex** or **display: inline-flex** property to a parent element. This property transforms the container's children into flex items, allowing developers to control their layout and behavior using various Flexbox properties.

cssCopy code

```
/* Example of creating a flex container */
.container { display: flex; /* Additional styling
properties */ }
```

In this example, the **.container** element becomes a flex container, and its child elements automatically become flex items.

One of the fundamental features of Flexbox is the ability to control the alignment of flex items along the main axis and cross axis of the flex container. The main axis is defined by the **flex-direction** property, which specifies whether the items should be laid out horizontally (**row** direction) or vertically (**column** direction).

cssCopy code

```
/* Example of setting the flex-direction */
.container { display: flex; flex-direction: row; /*
Horizontal layout */ }
```

By default, flex items align along the main axis according to their size and order. However, developers can use various alignment properties such as **justify-content** and **align-items** to control the alignment of items within the container.

cssCopy code

```
/* Example of aligning flex items */ .container {
display: flex; justify-content: center; /* Center-
align items along the main axis */ align-items:
center; /* Center-align items along the cross axis */
}
```

In this example, **justify-content: center** horizontally centers the flex items along the main axis, while

align-items: center vertically centers the items along the cross axis.

Flexbox also provides powerful features for controlling the size and flexibility of flex items. Developers can use properties such as **flex-grow**, **flex-shrink**, and **flex-basis** to specify how flex items should grow, shrink, and behave relative to each other within the flex container.

cssCopy code

/* Example of controlling flex item size */ .item { flex: 1; /* Grow, shrink, and basis */ }

In this example, the **.item** element is configured to grow and shrink equally (**flex: 1**), allowing it to fill any available space within the flex container.

Another essential feature of Flexbox is the ability to control the order of flex items using the **order** property. By default, flex items are displayed in the order they appear in the HTML markup. However, developers can use the **order** property to rearrange items dynamically without modifying the HTML structure.

cssCopy code

/* Example of changing the order of flex items */ .item-2 { order: 1; /* Move item to the beginning */ }

In this example, the **.item-2** element is given an order of **1**, causing it to be displayed before other items within the flex container.

In addition to these core features, Flexbox offers many other properties and capabilities for creating advanced layouts and designs. Developers can use properties such as **flex-wrap**, **align-content**, and **align-self** to control wrapping behavior, alignment of multiple lines of flex items, and individual alignment of flex items within the container.

cssCopy code

```
/* Example of controlling flex wrapping */
.container { display: flex; flex-wrap: wrap; /* Wrap items to multiple lines */ }
```

In this example, **flex-wrap: wrap** allows flex items to wrap to multiple lines within the flex container when they exceed the available space.

Overall, Flexbox provides developers with a powerful and intuitive layout model for creating responsive and dynamic web layouts. By understanding the essential concepts and properties of Flexbox, developers can efficiently design and implement flexible and adaptive layouts that enhance the user experience across various devices and screen sizes. Flexbox is a valuable tool in the modern web development toolkit, offering unparalleled flexibility and control over the layout and presentation of web content.

Advanced Flexbox techniques expand upon the foundational concepts of Flexbox layout to enable developers to create more complex and sophisticated layouts with greater precision and control. These techniques leverage the full power of Flexbox properties and features to address specific layout challenges and achieve desired design outcomes. Understanding and mastering these advanced techniques empowers developers to create dynamic, responsive, and visually compelling layouts that enhance the user experience and meet the demands of modern web design standards.

One of the advanced techniques in Flexbox is the use of the **flex-grow**, **flex-shrink**, and **flex-basis** properties in combination to precisely control the sizing and flexibility of flex items within a flex container. By adjusting these properties, developers can achieve fine-grained control over how flex items grow, shrink, and allocate space within the container, ensuring that layouts adapt seamlessly to varying content and viewport sizes.

cssCopy code

```
/* Example of advanced flex item sizing */ .item {
flex: 1 0 auto; /* Flex-grow, flex-shrink, flex-basis
*/ }
```

In this example, the **flex** property is used to specify a flex factor of **1**, indicating that the item can grow to fill available space, but should not shrink. The **auto** value for **flex-basis** instructs the item to use its natural width as the basis for flex calculations.

Another advanced technique involves using nested flex containers to create more complex and hierarchical layouts. By nesting flex containers within one another, developers can create multi-level layouts with different flex behaviors at each level, allowing for greater flexibility and control over the arrangement of elements within the overall layout structure.

htmlCopy code

```html
<!-- Example of nested flex containers --> <div class="outer-container"> <div class="inner-container"> <!-- Nested flex items --> </div> </div> <style> /* CSS for nested flex containers */ .outer-container { display: flex; /* Additional styling properties */ } .inner-container { display: flex; /* Additional styling properties */ } </style>
```

In this example, the **.outer-container** and **.inner-container** elements are both flex containers, allowing for independent control over the layout and alignment of their respective child elements.

Additionally, developers can leverage advanced alignment techniques such as **align-self** and **align-content** to control the alignment of individual flex items within a flex container and the alignment of multiple lines of flex items, respectively. These properties provide fine-grained control over the positioning and spacing of elements within complex layouts, ensuring that designs are visually consistent and aesthetically pleasing across different screen sizes and devices.

cssCopy code

```
/* Example of advanced alignment techniques */
.item { align-self: flex-start; /* Align individual item */ } .container { align-content: space-between; /* Align multiple lines of items */ }
```

In this example, the **align-self** property is used to align an individual flex item to the start of its cross axis, while the **align-content** property aligns multiple lines of items with equal spacing between them.

Furthermore, advanced Flexbox techniques include the use of flexbox ordering to dynamically reposition flex items based on specific layout requirements or user interactions. By adjusting the **order** property of flex items, developers can change their display order without modifying the HTML markup, providing greater flexibility and control over the layout presentation.

cssCopy code

```
/* Example of flexbox ordering */ .item-2 { order: 1; /* Move item to a different position */ }
```

In this example, the **.item-2** element is given an order of **1**, causing it to be displayed in a different position within the flex container compared to its original order in the HTML markup.

In summary, advanced Flexbox techniques build upon the foundational principles of Flexbox layout to provide developers with greater flexibility, precision, and control over the creation of complex and responsive web layouts. By mastering these techniques, developers can create sophisticated and visually stunning layouts that adapt seamlessly to different content and device contexts, enhancing the overall user experience and usability of web applications. Advanced Flexbox techniques are essential tools in the modern web developer's toolkit, enabling the creation of dynamic and engaging web experiences that meet the evolving demands of today's digital landscape.

Chapter 7: Grid Systems for Advanced Layouts

CSS Grid Layout, often referred to simply as Grid, is a powerful layout system that allows developers to create complex two-dimensional grid-based layouts with ease. Unlike Flexbox, which is primarily designed for one-dimensional layouts, CSS Grid enables developers to define both rows and columns within a grid container, providing a comprehensive solution for creating intricate and responsive layouts. With CSS Grid, developers can achieve precise control over the placement and alignment of elements within the grid, making it an indispensable tool for building modern web interfaces.

To begin using CSS Grid, developers must first define a grid container by applying the **display: grid** property to a parent element. This property transforms the container into a grid context, allowing developers to define rows and columns to organize the layout of its child elements.

cssCopy code

```
/* Example of creating a grid container */
.container { display: grid; /* Additional grid
properties */ }
```

In this example, the **.container** element becomes a grid container, and its child elements can be placed within the grid using grid-specific properties.

One of the defining features of CSS Grid is its ability to create a grid structure with rows and columns of varying sizes and alignments. Developers can use properties such as **grid-template-rows** and **grid-template-columns** to define the size and alignment of rows and columns within the grid, allowing for flexible and responsive layouts.

cssCopy code

```
/* Example of defining grid rows and columns */
.container { display: grid; grid-template-rows:
100px 200px; /* Two rows with specific heights */
grid-template-columns: 1fr 2fr; /* Two columns
with fractional widths */ }
```

In this example, the **.container** element is configured with two rows, the first with a height of **100px** and the second with a height of **200px**, and two columns with widths proportional to each other (1:2 ratio).

CSS Grid also offers powerful alignment and spacing capabilities, allowing developers to control the positioning and spacing of grid items within the grid container. Properties such as **justify-items, align-items, justify-content**, and **align-content** enable developers to align items along the grid's axes and distribute space within the grid container as needed.

cssCopy code

```css
/* Example of aligning grid items */ .container {
display: grid; justify-items: center; /* Center-align
items horizontally */ align-items: center; /*
Center-align items vertically */ justify-content:
space-around; /* Distribute extra space around
items */ align-content: space-between; /*
Distribute extra space between rows */ }
```

In this example, grid items within the **.container** element are centered both horizontally and vertically, and extra space is evenly distributed around items and between rows.

Moreover, CSS Grid supports the concept of grid tracks, which are the spaces between rows and columns within the grid. Developers can use properties such as **grid-gap, grid-row-gap**, and **grid-column-gap** to specify the size of these gaps, controlling the spacing between grid items and improving the overall readability and aesthetics of the layout.

cssCopy code

```css
/* Example of defining grid gaps */ .container {
display: grid; grid-gap: 20px; /* Set a uniform gap
between rows and columns */ grid-row-gap:
10px; /* Set a gap between rows */ grid-column-
gap: 15px; /* Set a gap between columns */ }
```

In this example, the **.container** element is configured with uniform gaps of **20px** between rows and columns, as well as specific gaps of **10px** between rows and **15px** between columns.

Additionally, CSS Grid provides robust support for responsive design, allowing developers to create layouts that adapt gracefully to different screen sizes and device orientations. By combining CSS Grid with media queries and other responsive design techniques, developers can create layouts that seamlessly adjust to the available viewport space, providing users with an optimal viewing experience across a wide range of devices and screen resolutions.

cssCopy code

```css
/* Example of responsive grid layout */ .container {
display: grid; grid-template-columns: repeat(auto-
fit, minmax(200px, 1fr)); /* Responsive columns
*/ } @media screen and (max-width: 768px) {
.container { grid-template-columns: repeat(2,
1fr); /* Two columns on smaller screens */ } }
```

In this example, the **.container** element is configured with a responsive grid layout that dynamically adjusts the number of columns based on the available viewport width. On smaller screens (max-width: 768px), the layout switches to a two-column grid to ensure optimal readability and usability.

In summary, CSS Grid is a powerful and versatile layout system that empowers developers to create sophisticated and responsive web layouts with ease. By providing robust support for grid-based layouts, alignment, spacing, and responsiveness, CSS Grid enables developers to build visually stunning and user-friendly interfaces that adapt seamlessly to different devices and screen sizes. Understanding the fundamentals of CSS Grid and mastering its advanced techniques is essential for modern web development, as it provides a comprehensive solution for building complex and flexible layouts that meet the evolving demands of web design standards.

Building complex layouts with CSS Grid is a fundamental aspect of modern web development, allowing developers to create sophisticated and visually appealing designs that adapt seamlessly to various screen sizes and device orientations. CSS Grid provides a powerful and intuitive way to structure and organize content within a grid-based layout, offering precise control over the placement and alignment of elements. By leveraging the features and capabilities of CSS Grid, developers can design complex and intricate layouts that enhance the user experience and improve the usability of web applications.

To begin building complex layouts with CSS Grid, developers must first understand the basic concepts and properties of the CSS Grid layout system. This includes defining a grid container using the **display: grid** property and specifying the structure of the grid using properties such as **grid-template-rows** and **grid-template-columns**.

cssCopy code

```
/* Example of defining grid rows and columns */
.container { display: grid; grid-template-rows: 100px 200px; /* Two rows with specific heights */ grid-template-columns: 1fr 2fr; /* Two columns with fractional widths */ }
```

In this example, the **.container** element is configured with two rows, each with a specific height, and two columns with fractional widths. This provides a basic grid structure for organizing content within the layout.

One of the key advantages of CSS Grid is its ability to handle complex layout scenarios, such as nested grids and grid item alignment. Nested grids allow developers to create hierarchical layouts with multiple levels of grid containers, providing greater flexibility and control over the arrangement of elements within the layout.

htmlCopy code

```
<!-- Example of nested grid containers --> <div class="outer-container"> <div class="inner-container"> <!-- Nested grid items --> </div> </div> <style> /* CSS for nested grid containers */ .outer-container { display: grid; /* Additional styling
```

properties */ } .inner-container { display: grid; /* Additional styling properties */ } </style>

In this example, both the **.outer-container** and **.inner-container** elements are grid containers, allowing for independent control over the layout and alignment of their respective child elements.

Furthermore, CSS Grid provides powerful alignment and spacing capabilities, enabling developers to precisely control the positioning and spacing of grid items within the grid container. Properties such as **justify-items**, **align-items**, **justify-content**, and **align-content** allow developers to align items along the grid's axes and distribute space within the container as needed.

cssCopy code

/* Example of aligning grid items */ .container { display: grid; justify-items: center; /* Center-align items horizontally */ align-items: center; /* Center-align items vertically */ justify-content: space-around; /* Distribute extra space around items */ align-content: space-between; /* Distribute extra space between rows */ }

In this example, grid items within the **.container** element are centered both horizontally and vertically, and extra space is evenly distributed around items and between rows.

Moreover, CSS Grid supports advanced features such as grid areas, named grid lines, and grid templates, which further enhance the capabilities of the layout system and enable developers to create complex and intricate designs with ease. Grid areas allow developers to define named regions within the grid layout, making it easier to place elements within specific areas of the grid.

cssCopy code

```
/* Example of defining grid areas */ .container {
display: grid; grid-template-areas: "header header"
"sidebar content" "footer footer"; }
```

In this example, the **.container** element is configured with named grid areas for the header, sidebar, content, and footer sections of the layout. This allows developers to easily position elements within these areas using the **grid-area** property.

Additionally, named grid lines enable developers to reference specific grid lines within the layout, making it easier to position elements relative to each other or to the edges of the grid container.

cssCopy code

```
/* Example of referencing named grid lines */ .item
{ grid-row: header-start / footer-end; /* Span from
header to footer */ grid-column: sidebar-start /
content-end; /* Span from sidebar to content */ }
```

In this example, the **.item** element is positioned to span from the header to the footer and from the sidebar to the content section of the layout using named grid lines.

Furthermore, CSS Grid templates allow developers to define complex grid structures with a concise and expressive syntax, making it easier to create intricate layouts with minimal code.

cssCopy code

```
/* Example of using grid templates */ .container {
display: grid; grid-template: "header header
header" "sidebar content content" "footer footer
footer" / 1fr 2fr 1fr; }
```

In this example, the **.container** element is configured with a grid template that defines three rows and three columns, with specific widths for each column.

Overall, building complex layouts with CSS Grid offers developers a flexible and powerful solution for creating modern web interfaces that meet the demands of today's digital landscape. By leveraging the features and capabilities of CSS Grid, developers can design sophisticated and visually appealing layouts that enhance the user experience and improve the usability of web applications. With its intuitive syntax and comprehensive set of features, CSS Grid is a valuable tool for building complex and responsive layouts that adapt seamlessly to different screen sizes and device orientations.

Chapter 8: Responsive Design with Media Queries

Media queries are a cornerstone of responsive web design, allowing developers to tailor the presentation of content based on various factors such as screen size, device orientation, and resolution. They enable websites to adapt dynamically to different viewing environments, providing users with an optimal browsing experience across a wide range of devices, from desktop computers to smartphones and tablets.

At their core, media queries consist of a media type and one or more expressions that define the conditions under which the styles within the query should apply. The most common media types include **all**, **screen**, **print**, **speech**, and **tv**, each targeting specific output devices or media types. For instance, the **screen** media type is commonly used for styles intended for display on screens, while **print** is used for print stylesheets.

cssCopy code

```
/* Example of a media query targeting screens with a maximum width */ @media screen and (max-width: 768px) { /* CSS styles for smaller screens */ }
```

In this example, the media query targets screens with a maximum width of **768px**, applying the specified styles when the screen size meets the defined condition.

Media queries can be applied using CSS in a separate stylesheet or directly within an HTML document using the **<style>** element. Additionally, they can be used inline within HTML elements, although this approach is less common and generally not recommended for maintainability reasons.

htmlCopy code

```
<!-- Example of an inline media query within an
HTML document --> <div style="color: red; @media
screen and (max-width: 768px) { color: blue; }">
This text changes color based on screen width.
</div>
```

While media queries are most commonly used to adjust styles based on screen size, they can also target other characteristics such as device orientation (**portrait** or **landscape**), resolution (**min-resolution** and **max-resolution**), and aspect ratio (**aspect-ratio**).

cssCopy code

```
/* Example of a media query targeting devices in
landscape orientation */ @media screen and
(orientation: landscape) { /* CSS styles for
landscape orientation */ }
```

In this example, the media query applies styles specifically tailored for devices in landscape orientation.

Furthermore, media queries can be combined using logical operators such as **and, not**, and **only**, allowing for more complex conditions to be defined.

cssCopy code

```
/* Example of a media query combining multiple conditions */ @media screen and (max-width: 768px) and (orientation: portrait) { /* CSS styles for small screens in portrait orientation */ }
```

In this example, the media query targets screens with a maximum width of **768px** and a portrait orientation, applying the specified styles only when both conditions are met.

When working with media queries, it's essential to consider the mobile-first approach, where styles for smaller screens are defined first, and then progressively enhanced for larger screens using media queries. This approach ensures that the website's layout and design are optimized for mobile devices by default, with additional styles added as needed for larger screens.

cssCopy code

```
/* Example of a mobile-first media query */ /* Default styles for all screens */ body { font-size: 16px; } /* Media query for larger screens */ @media screen and (min-width: 768px) { /*
```

Additional styles for screens wider than 768px */
body { font-size: 18px; } }

In this example, the default font size is set to **16px**, and then increased to **18px** for screens wider than **768px** using a media query.

In addition to targeting specific screen sizes, media queries can also be used to address accessibility considerations, such as adjusting styles for users with visual impairments or disabilities. For example, media queries can be used to change font sizes, increase contrast, or modify layout to improve readability and usability for all users.

cssCopy code

```
/* Example of a media query for improved accessibility */ @media screen and (prefers-color-scheme: dark) { /* CSS styles for dark mode */ body { background-color: #121212; color: #ffffff; }
}
```

In this example, the media query targets devices that prefer a dark color scheme, applying styles that enhance readability in low-light environments.

Overall, media queries are a versatile tool that enables developers to create responsive and accessible web designs that adapt seamlessly to different devices and user preferences. By leveraging media queries effectively, developers can ensure that their websites provide a consistent and optimal user experience across various viewing environments, contributing to improved usability and user satisfaction.

Advanced media query strategies play a crucial role in modern web development, offering developers powerful techniques to create highly responsive and adaptable layouts that cater to a diverse range of devices and screen sizes. While basic media queries enable developers to target specific device characteristics such as screen width or orientation, advanced strategies allow for more nuanced and sophisticated approaches to designing responsive websites.

One advanced media query strategy involves using feature queries, also known as @supports rules, to detect browser support for specific CSS features before applying corresponding styles. This technique ensures that styles are only applied if the browser supports certain CSS properties or values, preventing potential layout issues or rendering inconsistencies in unsupported browsers.

cssCopy code

```
/* Example of a feature query */ /* Apply CSS Grid styles only if supported by the browser */ @supports (display: grid) { .container { display: grid; grid-template-columns: 1fr 1fr; /* Additional grid styles */ } }
```

In this example, the CSS Grid styles are only applied to the **.container** element if the browser supports the **display: grid** property, ensuring graceful degradation for browsers that do not support CSS Grid.

Another advanced media query strategy involves using custom media queries and variables to create reusable and modular styles that can be easily adapted and customized for different layouts or components. Custom media queries allow developers to define named breakpoints or conditions based on specific design requirements, making it easier to maintain and update responsive styles across multiple components or pages.

cssCopy code

```
/* Example of a custom media query */ /* Define
custom breakpoints using CSS variables */ :root { --
tablet: 768px; --desktop: 1024px; } /* Apply styles
for tablets and larger screens */ @media (min-
width: var(--tablet)) { /* Tablet and desktop styles
*/ .header { font-size: 20px; } } /* Apply styles for
desktop screens */ @media (min-width: var(--
desktop)) { /* Desktop-only styles */ .sidebar {
width: 250px; } }
```

In this example, custom CSS variables are used to define breakpoints for tablet and desktop screens, allowing for more flexible and modular media queries that can adapt to changing design requirements.

Additionally, advanced media query strategies often involve combining media queries with other CSS techniques such as grid systems, flexbox, or CSS frameworks to create complex and dynamic layouts that respond fluidly to different screen sizes and orientations. For example, developers can use CSS frameworks like Bootstrap or Tailwind CSS to streamline the process of building responsive layouts, leveraging predefined grid systems and utility classes to achieve consistent and scalable designs across various devices.

htmlCopy code

```html
<!-- Example of using a CSS framework for responsive layout --> <div class="container"> <div class="row"> <div class="col-md-6"> <!-- Content for medium-sized screens and larger --> </div> <div class="col-md-6"> <!-- Content for medium-sized screens and larger --> </div> </div> </div>
```

In this example, the Bootstrap grid system is used to create a responsive layout with two columns that stack vertically on smaller screens and display side-by-side on medium-sized screens and larger.

Moreover, advanced media query strategies often involve optimizing website performance and loading times by using techniques such as lazy loading or serving different image sizes based on screen resolution. By detecting the user's device capabilities and network conditions, developers can deliver optimized content and ensure a fast and seamless browsing experience across all devices.

htmlCopy code

```
<!-- Example of lazy loading images with the loading attribute --> <img src="image.jpg" alt="Image" loading="lazy">
```

In this example, the **loading="lazy"** attribute is added to the **<img>** element to enable lazy loading, allowing images to load asynchronously as the user scrolls down the page, reducing initial page load times and improving performance.

In summary, advanced media query strategies empower developers to create highly responsive and adaptable websites that deliver a seamless user experience across a wide range of devices and screen sizes. By leveraging feature queries, custom media queries, CSS frameworks, and performance optimization techniques, developers can build modern and efficient web applications that meet the demands of today's digital landscape.

Chapter 9: Transformations and Transitions

Understanding CSS transformations is essential for modern web development, as they allow developers to manipulate the appearance and layout of elements in creative and dynamic ways. Transformations enable elements to be scaled, rotated, skewed, and translated, providing flexibility in designing visually appealing and interactive user interfaces. By applying transformations, developers can enhance the user experience by adding engaging animations, creating responsive layouts, and implementing immersive visual effects.

One of the most commonly used CSS transformations is the **transform** property, which serves as the foundation for applying various types of transformations to HTML elements. The **transform** property accepts a variety of transformation functions, each with its own set of parameters that determine how the transformation is applied. These functions include **translate()**, **rotate()**, **scale()**, **skew()**, and **matrix()**, among others, allowing for precise control over the transformation effects.

cssCopy code

```
/* Example of applying a translation transformation */ .element { transform: translate(50px, 50px); }
```

In this example, the **.element** is translated 50 pixels horizontally and 50 pixels vertically from its original position.

Transformations can also be combined and chained together to create more complex effects. By applying multiple transformation functions within the **transform** property, developers can achieve sophisticated transformations that alter the appearance and behavior of elements in intricate ways.

cssCopy code

```
/* Example of combining multiple transformations */ .element { transform: rotate(45deg) scale(1.5) skewX(20deg); }
```

In this example, the **.element** is rotated by 45 degrees, scaled to 150% of its original size, and skewed horizontally by 20 degrees.

In addition to 2D transformations, CSS also supports 3D transformations, allowing elements to be transformed in three-dimensional space. 3D transformations enable developers to create more realistic and immersive effects by adding depth and perspective to elements. To apply 3D transformations, developers can use functions such as **rotateX()**, **rotateY()**, **rotateZ()**, **translate3d()**, and **scale3d()**.

cssCopy code

```css
/* Example of applying a 3D rotation transformation
*/ .element { transform: rotateY(45deg); }
```

In this example, the **.element** is rotated around the y-axis by 45 degrees, creating a 3D rotation effect.

Furthermore, CSS transformations can be animated using CSS animations or transitions, allowing for smooth and fluid transitions between different states or positions. By animating transformations, developers can create visually engaging effects that capture the user's attention and enhance the overall user experience.

cssCopy code

```css
/* Example of animating a transformation */
.element { transition: transform 0.3s ease-in-out; }
.element:hover { transform: scale(1.2); }
```

In this example, the **.element** scales to 120% of its original size with a smooth transition when hovered over, creating a simple but effective animation effect.

When working with CSS transformations, it's important to consider browser compatibility and performance implications. While modern web browsers support CSS transformations, certain older browsers may not fully support all transformation features, requiring fallback options or alternative approaches for achieving similar effects. Additionally, complex transformations or animations may impact page performance, particularly on mobile devices with limited processing power and memory.

To ensure cross-browser compatibility and optimize performance, developers can use feature detection techniques to detect browser support for specific transformation features and provide fallback options for unsupported browsers. Additionally, developers can optimize performance by minimizing the number of elements being transformed, using hardware-accelerated rendering when available, and avoiding unnecessary or overly complex transformations.

In summary, understanding CSS transformations is essential for creating visually appealing and interactive web experiences. By leveraging transformations, developers can manipulate the appearance and layout of elements with precision and creativity, adding depth, dimension, and dynamism to web pages. Whether used for animating user interface elements, designing responsive layouts, or implementing immersive visual effects, CSS transformations offer a versatile and powerful toolset for modern web development.

Transition effects in CSS are a fundamental aspect of modern web development, enabling developers to create smooth and visually appealing animations that enhance user interactions and improve the overall user experience. With CSS transitions, developers can animate the change in CSS properties over a specified duration, allowing for seamless transitions between different states or styles. Transition effects can be applied to various elements and properties, including color, size, position, opacity, and more, providing endless possibilities for creating engaging animations and effects.

The key to understanding CSS transitions lies in the **transition** property, which allows developers to define the CSS properties to be animated, the duration of the animation, the timing function that controls the animation's acceleration and deceleration, and any delay before the animation starts. By specifying these parameters, developers can create animations that smoothly transition from one state to another, adding polish and finesse to web interfaces.

cssCopy code

```css
/* Example of applying a transition effect */
.element { transition: background-color 0.3s ease-in-out; } .element:hover { background-color: #ff0000; }
```

In this example, the background color of the **.element** smoothly transitions to red (**#ff0000**) over a duration of **0.3s** with an easing function that accelerates and decelerates the animation.

Easing functions play a crucial role in controlling the timing and pacing of CSS transitions, allowing developers to create animations with different levels of smoothness and realism. Common easing functions include **ease, ease-in, ease-out, ease-in-out, linear**, and various custom cubic-bezier functions, each offering unique acceleration and deceleration profiles.

cssCopy code

```
/* Example of using different easing functions */
.element { transition: opacity 0.5s ease-in-out; }
.element:hover { opacity: 0; }
```

In this example, the opacity of the **.element** smoothly transitions to **0** (fully transparent) over a duration of **0.5s** with an easing function that accelerates and decelerates the animation.

Moreover, CSS transitions can be combined with other CSS features such as pseudo-classes, media queries, and keyframe animations to create more complex and dynamic effects. By chaining transitions with hover states, for example, developers can trigger animations in response to user interactions, providing instant visual feedback and improving usability.

cssCopy code

```
/* Example of combining transitions with hover states */ .element { transition: transform 0.3s
```

ease-in-out; } .element:hover { transform:
scale(1.2); }

In this example, the **.element** scales to **120%** of its
original size with a smooth transition when hovered
over, creating a simple but effective animation
effect.

Furthermore, CSS transitions are not limited to
single-property animations; developers can animate
multiple properties simultaneously by comma-
separating property declarations within the
transition property. This allows for more complex
and synchronized animations, enhancing the
richness and interactivity of web interfaces.

cssCopy code

```
/* Example of animating multiple properties */
.element { transition: background-color 0.3s ease-
in-out, transform 0.3s ease-in-out; }
.element:hover { background-color: #ff0000;
transform: scale(1.2); }
```

In this example, the **.element** smoothly transitions
its background color to red and scales to **120%** of its
original size when hovered over, with both
animations occurring simultaneously over a
duration of **0.3s** with an easing function that
accelerates and decelerates the animation.

When deploying CSS transitions in real-world
projects, it's important to consider browser
compatibility and performance implications. While

modern web browsers generally support CSS transitions, certain older browsers may not fully support all transition features, requiring fallback options or alternative approaches for achieving similar effects. Additionally, complex or excessive use of transitions may impact page performance, particularly on mobile devices with limited processing power and memory.

To ensure cross-browser compatibility and optimize performance, developers can use feature detection techniques to detect browser support for specific transition features and provide fallback options for unsupported browsers. Additionally, developers can optimize performance by minimizing the number of elements being animated, using hardware-accelerated rendering when available, and avoiding unnecessary or overly complex animations.

In summary, CSS transitions are a powerful tool for creating smooth and visually appealing animations in web development. By leveraging transitions, developers can enhance user interactions, provide instant feedback, and improve the overall user experience of web applications. With careful planning and consideration of browser compatibility and performance considerations, CSS transitions offer a versatile and effective way to add polish and finesse to web interfaces.

Chapter 10: Animations and Keyframes

Introduction to CSS animations is an essential aspect of modern web development, offering developers powerful tools to create dynamic and engaging user experiences. CSS animations allow elements on a webpage to move, change size, fade in or out, and perform other transformations over time, without the need for JavaScript or external libraries. With CSS animations, developers can bring websites to life, capturing users' attention and enhancing usability.

The foundation of CSS animations lies in the **@keyframes** rule, which defines the sequence of styles to be applied to an element at various stages of the animation. Using keyframes, developers specify the starting and ending states of an animation, as well as any intermediate states, allowing for precise control over the animation's behavior and appearance.

cssCopy code

```
/* Example of defining keyframes for an animation */ @keyframes slide-in { 0% { transform: translateX(-100%); } 100% { transform: translateX(0); } }
```

In this example, the **slide-in** animation moves an element from left to right by translating it horizontally (**transform: translateX()**) from **-100%** to **0%** of its container's width.

Once the keyframes are defined, developers can apply the animation to an element using the **animation** property, specifying the name of the keyframes (**slide-in**), the duration of the animation, the timing function, any delay before the animation starts, and whether the animation should repeat or alternate.

cssCopy code

```
/* Example of applying an animation to an element
*/ .element { animation: slide-in 1s ease-out
forwards; }
```

In this example, the **.element** animates using the **slide-in** keyframes over a duration of **1s**, with an easing function that decelerates towards the end (**ease-out**), and the animation state persists after completion (**forwards**).

CSS animations offer a wide range of possibilities for creating visually stunning effects and interactions on the web. Developers can animate various CSS properties, including position, size, color, opacity, and rotation, allowing for endless creativity in designing animations.

cssCopy code

```
/* Example of animating multiple properties */
@keyframes pulse { 0% { transform: scale(1);
opacity: 1; } 50% { transform: scale(1.2); opacity:
```

0.5; } 100% { transform: scale(1); opacity: 1; } }
.element { animation: pulse 2s infinite; }

In this example, the **pulse** animation scales and changes the opacity of the **.element** to create a pulsating effect, with the animation repeating indefinitely (**infinite**) over a duration of **2s**.

CSS animations can also be combined with other CSS features, such as transitions, transforms, and pseudo-classes, to create more complex and dynamic effects. By chaining animations with hover states, for example, developers can trigger animations in response to user interactions, providing engaging and interactive experiences.

cssCopy code

```
/* Example of combining animations with hover states */ @keyframes shake { 0% { transform: translateX(0); } 50% { transform: translateX(-10px); } 100% { transform: translateX(10px); } }
.element { animation: shake 0.5s ease-in-out infinite; } .element:hover { animation: none; }
```

In this example, the **shake** animation moves the **.element** horizontally (**transform: translateX()**) from side to side, creating a shaking effect. The animation repeats infinitely (**infinite**) over a duration of **0.5s** with an easing function that accelerates and decelerates (**ease-in-out**). When hovered over, the animation is paused (**animation:**

none;), providing a responsive and interactive experience.

When deploying CSS animations in real-world projects, it's important to consider browser compatibility and performance implications. While modern web browsers generally support CSS animations, certain older browsers may not fully support all animation features, requiring fallback options or alternative approaches for achieving similar effects. Additionally, complex or excessive use of animations may impact page performance, particularly on mobile devices with limited processing power and memory.

To ensure cross-browser compatibility and optimize performance, developers can use feature detection techniques to detect browser support for specific animation features and provide fallback options for unsupported browsers. Additionally, developers can optimize performance by minimizing the number and complexity of animations, using hardware-accelerated rendering when available, and employing techniques such as lazy loading and requestAnimationFrame for smoother animations.

In summary, introduction to CSS animations opens up a world of possibilities for creating dynamic and engaging web experiences. With CSS animations, developers can bring websites to life, capturing users' attention and enhancing usability. By mastering the fundamentals of CSS animations and exploring advanced techniques, developers can create visually stunning effects and interactions that elevate the quality and impact of their web projects.

Creating keyframe animations in CSS is a pivotal skill for modern web developers, as it allows them to bring websites to life with captivating and dynamic animations. Keyframe animations provide developers with precise control over the animation's behavior and appearance, enabling them to define custom sequences of styles that dictate how an element changes over time. By mastering keyframe animations, developers can create visually stunning effects that enhance the user experience and set their websites apart from the competition.

The foundation of keyframe animations lies in the **@keyframes** rule, which allows developers to define a set of keyframes representing various stages of the animation. Each keyframe specifies the styles that should be applied to the element at a particular point in time during the animation. By defining multiple keyframes and specifying the desired styles for each, developers can create complex animations with smooth transitions between different states.

cssCopy code

```
/* Example of defining keyframes for a simple animation */ @keyframes slide-in { 0% {
```

transform: translateX(-100%); } 100% { transform: translateX(0); } }

In this example, the **slide-in** animation moves an element from left to right by translating it horizontally (**transform: translateX()**) from **-100%** to **0%** of its container's width.

Once the keyframes are defined, developers can apply the animation to an element using the **animation** property, specifying the name of the keyframes (**slide-in**), the duration of the animation, the timing function, any delay before the animation starts, and whether the animation should repeat or alternate.

cssCopy code

```
/* Example of applying an animation to an element */ .element { animation: slide-in 1s ease-out forwards; }
```

In this example, the **.element** animates using the **slide-in** keyframes over a duration of **1s**, with an easing function that decelerates towards the end (**ease-out**), and the animation state persists after completion (**forwards**).

Keyframe animations offer a wide range of possibilities for creating visually stunning effects and interactions on the web. Developers can animate various CSS properties, including position, size, color, opacity, and rotation, allowing for endless creativity in designing animations.

cssCopy code

```css
/* Example of a more complex animation with
multiple keyframes */ @keyframes pulse { 0% {
transform: scale(1); opacity: 1; } 50% {
transform: scale(1.2); opacity: 0.5; } 100% {
transform: scale(1); opacity: 1; } } .element {
animation: pulse 2s infinite; }
```

In this example, the **pulse** animation scales and changes the opacity of the **.element** to create a pulsating effect, with the animation repeating indefinitely (**infinite**) over a duration of **2s**.

Keyframe animations can also be combined with other CSS features, such as transitions, transforms, and pseudo-classes, to create more complex and dynamic effects. By chaining animations with hover states, for example, developers can trigger animations in response to user interactions, providing engaging and interactive experiences.

cssCopy code

```css
/* Example of combining animations with hover
states */ @keyframes shake { 0% { transform:
translateX(0); } 50% { transform: translateX(-
10px); } 100% { transform: translateX(10px); } }
.element { animation: shake 0.5s ease-in-out
infinite; } .element:hover { animation: none; }
```

In this example, the **shake** animation moves the **.element** horizontally (**transform: translateX()**)

194

from side to side, creating a shaking effect. The animation repeats infinitely (**infinite**) over a duration of **0.5s** with an easing function that accelerates and decelerates (**ease-in-out**). When hovered over, the animation is paused (**animation: none;**), providing a responsive and interactive experience.

When deploying keyframe animations in real-world projects, it's important to consider browser compatibility and performance implications. While modern web browsers generally support keyframe animations, certain older browsers may not fully support all animation features, requiring fallback options or alternative approaches for achieving similar effects. Additionally, complex or excessive use of animations may impact page performance, particularly on mobile devices with limited processing power and memory.

To ensure cross-browser compatibility and optimize performance, developers can use feature detection techniques to detect browser support for specific animation features and provide fallback options for unsupported browsers. Additionally, developers can optimize performance by minimizing the number and complexity of animations, using hardware-accelerated rendering when available, and employing techniques such as lazy loading and requestAnimationFrame for smoother animations.

In summary, creating keyframe animations in CSS is a powerful technique for adding dynamic and engaging effects to websites. By mastering keyframe animations and exploring advanced techniques, developers can create visually stunning animations that enhance the user experience and elevate the quality of their web projects.

Chapter 11: Customizing Forms and Inputs

Styling form elements is a crucial aspect of web development, as forms are integral components of many websites and applications, facilitating user interaction and data submission. By applying CSS styles to form elements, developers can enhance the visual appearance and usability of forms, ensuring they align with the overall design aesthetic of the website and provide a seamless user experience.

When styling form elements, developers can target various HTML input types, such as text inputs, checkboxes, radio buttons, dropdown menus, and buttons, each requiring unique styling approaches to achieve the desired look and feel. CSS selectors allow developers to target specific elements or groups of elements within a form, applying styles to customize their appearance, size, spacing, and behavior.

cssCopy code

```
/* Example of styling a text input */
input[type="text"] { width: 100%; padding: 10px;
border: 1px solid #ccc; border-radius: 5px; font-
size: 16px; } /* Example of styling a submit button
*/ input[type="submit"] { background-color:
```

#007bff; color: #fff; padding: 10px 20px; border: none; border-radius: 5px; font-size: 16px; cursor: pointer; }

In this example, the **input[type="text"]** selector targets text input elements, applying styles to set their width, padding, border, border radius, font size, and other properties. Similarly, the **input[type="submit"]** selector targets submit button elements, customizing their background color, text color, padding, border, border radius, font size, and cursor style.

In addition to targeting specific input types, developers can use pseudo-classes and pseudo-elements to style form elements based on their states, such as **:hover**, **:focus**, **:checked**, and **::placeholder**, allowing for dynamic styling based on user interactions or input values.

cssCopy code

/* Example of styling a button on hover */ button:hover { background-color: #0056b3; } /* Example of styling a checkbox label */ input[type="checkbox"] + label::before { content: "\2714"; margin-right: 5px; }

In this example, the **button:hover** selector changes the background color of a button when hovered over by the user, providing visual feedback. The **input[type="checkbox"] + label::before** selector inserts a checkmark symbol before the label text of a checkbox, enhancing its appearance.

Furthermore, developers can leverage CSS frameworks, such as Bootstrap, Foundation, or Materialize, which provide pre-designed styles and components for form elements, streamlining the styling process and ensuring consistency across different projects.

htmlCopy code

```html
<!-- Example of using Bootstrap styles for form elements --> <div class="form-group"> <label for="exampleInputEmail1">Email address</label> <input type="email" class="form-control" id="exampleInputEmail1" aria-describedby="emailHelp" placeholder="Enter email"> <small id="emailHelp" class="form-text text-muted">We'll never share your email with anyone else.</small> </div>
```

In this example, the Bootstrap classes **form-group**, **form-control**, and **form-text** are applied to the form elements to style them according to Bootstrap's design guidelines, providing a modern and consistent appearance.

When deploying styled form elements in a web project, developers should ensure cross-browser compatibility and accessibility, as different browsers and assistive technologies may interpret CSS styles differently. Testing and validation are essential steps to ensure that styled form elements function as expected and remain accessible to all users, including those with disabilities.

In summary, styling form elements with CSS is a fundamental skill for web developers, allowing them to customize the appearance and behavior of forms to meet the specific requirements of their projects. By leveraging CSS selectors, pseudo-classes, pseudo-elements, and frameworks, developers can create visually appealing and user-friendly forms that enhance the overall user experience of their websites and applications.

Custom form design techniques are essential for web developers to create unique and user-friendly forms that align with the overall design aesthetic of a website or application. By employing CSS, JavaScript, and HTML techniques, developers can customize form elements, layouts, and interactions to enhance usability and improve the user experience.

One common approach to custom form design is to style form elements using CSS to match the visual design of the website or application. CSS provides a wide range of properties and selectors that allow developers to customize the appearance of form inputs, labels, buttons, and other elements. For example, developers can use CSS to change the color, size, font, padding, and border of form elements, ensuring they blend seamlessly with the rest of the design.

cssCopy code

```css
/* Example of customizing form inputs with CSS */
input[type="text"], input[type="email"], input[type="password"] { width: 100%; padding: 10px; border: 1px solid #ccc; border-radius: 5px; font-size: 16px; margin-bottom: 10px; }
```

In this example, CSS is used to style text, email, and password input fields with consistent padding, borders, and font sizes, ensuring a cohesive look across different types of inputs.

Another technique for custom form design is to use JavaScript to enhance form interactions and validation. JavaScript can be used to create custom form validation rules, handle form submissions asynchronously, and provide real-time feedback to users as they fill out the form. For example, developers can use JavaScript to validate email addresses, passwords, and other input fields, ensuring they meet specific criteria before allowing the form to be submitted.

javascriptCopy code

```javascript
// Example of custom form validation with JavaScript const form = document.getElementById('myForm');
form.addEventListener('submit', function(event) {
const emailInput =
```

```
document.getElementById('email');           const
passwordInput                                 =
document.getElementById('password');          if
(!isValidEmail(emailInput.value))             {
event.preventDefault(); alert('Please enter a valid
email       address.');      return;      }      if
(!isValidPassword(passwordInput.value))        {
event.preventDefault(); alert('Password must be
at least 8 characters long.'); return; } }); function
isValidEmail(email) { // Regular expression for
validating email addresses const emailRegex =
/^[^\s@]+@[^\s@]+\.[^\s@]+$/;                return
emailRegex.test(email);        }         function
isValidPassword(password)        {          return
password.length >= 8; }
```

In this example, JavaScript is used to add custom validation logic to a form, checking whether the email address and password meet specific requirements before allowing the form to be submitted.

Additionally, developers can use HTML techniques such as custom form elements, semantic markup, and accessibility features to improve the usability and accessibility of forms. HTML5 introduced new input types, attributes, and elements that allow developers to create more user-friendly and accessible forms. For example, developers can use the **<label>** element to associate labels with form inputs, making it easier for users to understand the purpose of each input field.

htmlCopy code

```
<!-- Example of using semantic markup for form elements --> <form> <label for="email">Email:</label> <input type="email" id="email" name="email" required> <label for="password">Password:</label> <input type="password" id="password" name="password" required> <button type="submit">Submit</button> </form>
```

In this example, the **<label>** element is used to provide labels for the email and password input fields, improving accessibility and usability for users who rely on screen readers or other assistive technologies.

Furthermore, developers can leverage CSS frameworks and libraries such as Bootstrap, Foundation, or Materialize to streamline the process of designing and styling custom forms. These frameworks provide pre-designed form components, styles, and layout grids that developers can use to quickly create responsive and visually appealing forms with minimal effort.

htmlCopy code

```
<!-- Example of using Bootstrap for custom form design --> <form class="container"> <div
```

```html
class="form-group">                    <label
for="exampleInputEmail1">Email   address</label>
<input      type="email"      class="form-control"
id="exampleInputEmail1"                      aria-
describedby="emailHelp"      placeholder="Enter
email">   <small  id="emailHelp"  class="form-text
text-muted">We'll  never  share  your  email  with
anyone  else.</small>  </div>  <div  class="form-
group">                                          <label
for="exampleInputPassword1">Password</label>
<input    type="password"    class="form-control"
id="exampleInputPassword1"
placeholder="Password">      </div>      <button
type="submit"        class="btn           btn-
primary">Submit</button> </form>
```

In this example, Bootstrap classes are used to style form elements, labels, and buttons, providing a modern and responsive design for the form.

In summary, custom form design techniques are essential for creating user-friendly and visually appealing forms on the web. By combining CSS, JavaScript, and HTML techniques, developers can customize form elements, interactions, and validations to meet the specific requirements of their projects while ensuring a seamless and intuitive user experience. Whether styling form elements with CSS, adding custom validation with JavaScript, or leveraging HTML features and frameworks, custom form design plays a crucial role in enhancing the usability and accessibility of web forms.

Chapter 12: Optimization and Performance in CSS

CSS performance best practices are crucial for ensuring that web pages load quickly and efficiently, providing users with a smooth browsing experience. By optimizing CSS code and implementing best practices, developers can reduce page load times, minimize render-blocking resources, and improve overall website performance.

One key best practice is to minimize the number of CSS files and reduce their file size by removing unnecessary code and comments. Combining multiple CSS files into a single file using tools like Sass or Less can help reduce HTTP requests and improve loading times. Additionally, minifying CSS files by removing whitespace, comments, and unnecessary characters can further reduce file size and improve performance.

bashCopy code

Example of using Sass to compile and minify CSS files sass input.scss output.min.css --style compressed

In this example, Sass is used to compile an input SCSS file into a minified CSS file with the **compressed** style option, removing unnecessary whitespace and comments to reduce file size.

Another best practice is to leverage CSS specificity and inheritance to minimize redundancy and optimize stylesheets. Avoid using overly specific selectors or inline styles, as they can increase file size and make it harder to maintain and update stylesheets. Instead, use class-based selectors and inheritance to apply styles consistently across multiple elements.

cssCopy code

```
/* Example of using class-based selectors */
.button { background-color: #007bff; color: #fff; padding: 10px 20px; border: none; border-radius: 5px; font-size: 16px; } /* Example of using inheritance */ .container { font-family: Arial, sans-serif; font-size: 16px; } .container p { color: #333; }
```

In this example, class-based selectors are used to apply button styles consistently across multiple buttons, while inheritance is used to apply font styles to paragraph elements within a container.

Additionally, developers should prioritize critical CSS and load essential stylesheets inline or asynchronously to improve page rendering performance. Critical CSS refers to the styles required to render above-the-fold content, such as headers, navigation menus, and hero sections. By inlining critical CSS directly into the HTML or asynchronously loading non-critical stylesheets, developers can optimize page load times and improve perceived performance.

htmlCopy code

```
<!-- Example of inlining critical CSS --> <head>
<style> /* Critical CSS styles */ .header {
background-color: #007bff; color: #fff; } .nav { ... } /*
Other non-critical stylesheets loaded
asynchronously */ <link rel="preload"
href="styles.css" as="style"
onload="this.onload=null;this.rel='stylesheet'">
<noscript><link rel="stylesheet"
href="styles.css"></noscript> </style> </head>
```

In this example, critical CSS styles are inlined directly into the HTML head section, ensuring that above-the-fold content is styled without additional HTTP requests. Non-critical stylesheets are loaded asynchronously using the **<link>** element with the **preload** attribute to minimize render-blocking resources.

Furthermore, developers should optimize CSS animations and transitions to reduce rendering and painting times, especially on mobile devices. Avoid using expensive CSS properties or animating large numbers of elements simultaneously, as they can cause performance issues and degrade user experience. Instead, use hardware-accelerated properties like **transform** and **opacity**, and minimize layout changes to improve animation performance.

cssCopy code

```
/* Example of optimizing CSS animations */
.element { transition: transform 0.3s ease-out; }
.element:hover { transform: scale(1.1); }
```

In this example, the **transition** property is used to animate the **transform** property on hover, creating a smooth scaling effect with minimal impact on performance.

In summary, CSS performance best practices are essential for optimizing website performance and ensuring a seamless user experience. By minimizing CSS file size, leveraging specificity and inheritance, prioritizing critical CSS, and optimizing animations and transitions, developers can reduce page load times, improve rendering performance, and enhance overall website performance. By following these best practices, developers can create faster, more efficient websites that provide users with a smooth and enjoyable browsing experience.

Optimizing CSS for faster page loads is essential for improving website performance and providing users with a seamless browsing experience. By reducing CSS file size, minimizing render-blocking resources, and optimizing stylesheets, developers can significantly improve page load times and enhance overall website performance.

One effective technique for optimizing CSS is to minimize the number of CSS files and reduce their file size by removing unnecessary code and comments. Combining multiple CSS files into a single file using tools like Sass or Less can help reduce HTTP requests and improve loading times. Additionally, minifying CSS files by removing whitespace, comments, and unnecessary characters can further reduce file size and improve performance.

bashCopy code

```
# Example of using Sass to compile and minify CSS files sass input.scss output.min.css --style compressed
```

In this example, Sass is used to compile an input SCSS file into a minified CSS file with the **compressed** style option, removing unnecessary whitespace and comments to reduce file size.

Another optimization technique is to leverage CSS specificity and inheritance to minimize redundancy and optimize stylesheets. Avoid using overly specific selectors or inline styles, as they can increase file size and make it harder to maintain and update stylesheets. Instead, use class-based selectors and inheritance to apply styles consistently across multiple elements.

cssCopy code

```
/* Example of using class-based selectors */
.button { background-color: #007bff; color: #fff; padding: 10px 20px; border: none; border-radius: 5px; font-size: 16px; } /* Example of using
```

inheritance */ .container { font-family: Arial, sans-serif; font-size: 16px; } .container p { color: #333; }

In this example, class-based selectors are used to apply button styles consistently across multiple buttons, while inheritance is used to apply font styles to paragraph elements within a container.

Additionally, developers should prioritize critical CSS and load essential stylesheets inline or asynchronously to improve page rendering performance. Critical CSS refers to the styles required to render above-the-fold content, such as headers, navigation menus, and hero sections. By inlining critical CSS directly into the HTML or asynchronously loading non-critical stylesheets, developers can optimize page load times and improve perceived performance.

htmlCopy code

```
<!-- Example of inlining critical CSS --> <head>
<style> /* Critical CSS styles */ .header {
background-color: #007bff; color: #fff; } .nav { ... } /*
Other non-critical stylesheets loaded
asynchronously */ <link rel="preload"
href="styles.css" as="style"
onload="this.onload=null;this.rel='stylesheet'">
<noscript><link rel="stylesheet"
href="styles.css"></noscript> </style> </head>
```

In this example, critical CSS styles are inlined directly into the HTML head section, ensuring that above-the-fold content is styled without additional HTTP requests. Non-critical stylesheets are loaded asynchronously using the **<link>** element with the **preload** attribute to minimize render-blocking resources.

Furthermore, developers should optimize CSS animations and transitions to reduce rendering and painting times, especially on mobile devices. Avoid using expensive CSS properties or animating large numbers of elements simultaneously, as they can cause performance issues and degrade user experience. Instead, use hardware-accelerated properties like **transform** and **opacity**, and minimize layout changes to improve animation performance.

cssCopy code

```
/* Example of optimizing CSS animations */
.element { transition: transform 0.3s ease-out; }
.element:hover { transform: scale(1.1); }
```

In this example, the **transition** property is used to animate the **transform** property on hover, creating a smooth scaling effect with minimal impact on performance.

In summary, optimizing CSS for faster page loads is crucial for improving website performance and providing users with a smooth browsing experience. By reducing CSS file size, leveraging specificity and inheritance, prioritizing critical CSS, and optimizing animations and transitions, developers can significantly improve page load times and enhance overall website performance. By following these optimization techniques, developers can create faster, more efficient websites that deliver a seamless user experience.

BOOK 3
JAVASCRIPT WIZARDRY
ADVANCED TECHNIQUES FOR DYNAMIC WEB DEVELOPMENT

ROB BOTWRIGHT

Chapter 1: Introduction to JavaScript: Language Fundamentals

JavaScript, initially known as LiveScript, was conceived by Brendan Eich, a programmer at Netscape Communications Corporation, in September 1995. The language was developed to provide interactive features to the Netscape Navigator web browser. Its origins lie in the necessity to introduce client-side scripting to web pages, enabling developers to manipulate web content dynamically. Despite its humble beginnings, JavaScript has evolved significantly over the years, becoming one of the most widely used programming languages in the world today.

Initially released under the name LiveScript, the language was later renamed JavaScript as part of a partnership between Netscape and Sun Microsystems, leveraging the popularity of Java at the time. JavaScript 1.0 was introduced in March 1996, featuring core functionalities such as variables, control structures, and functions. However, its capabilities were limited compared to modern standards.

The release of JavaScript 1.1 in 1996 marked a significant milestone in the language's evolution, introducing new features such as regular expressions and better support for handling complex data types. Subsequent iterations, including JavaScript 1.2 and JavaScript 1.3, continued to enhance the language with features like exception handling and more robust object-oriented programming capabilities.

Despite its growing popularity, JavaScript faced challenges due to inconsistencies in browser implementations and lack of standardization. To address these issues, the European Computer Manufacturers Association (ECMA) developed a standardized specification for the language, known as ECMAScript. ECMAScript 1 was released in June 1997, providing a standardized foundation for JavaScript development.

Over the years, ECMAScript has undergone several revisions, introducing new features and improvements to the language. ECMAScript 3, released in December 1999, became the de facto standard for web development, offering significant enhancements such as regular expressions, exception handling, and improved support for object-oriented programming.

With the advent of Web 2.0 and the rise of dynamic web applications, JavaScript's importance grew exponentially. Frameworks and libraries like jQuery, AngularJS, and React emerged, revolutionizing web development by providing powerful tools and abstractions for building interactive and responsive user interfaces.

In 2015, ECMAScript 6 (ES6), also known as ECMAScript 2015, was released, introducing major enhancements to the language, including arrow functions, classes, modules, and enhanced syntax for working with arrays and objects. ES6 represented a significant leap forward for JavaScript, enabling developers to write more expressive and maintainable code.

Subsequent versions of ECMAScript, including ECMAScript 2016 (ES7) and ECMAScript 2017 (ES8), continued to introduce new features and improvements to the language. ES7 introduced features like async/await for asynchronous programming, while ES8 introduced features such as async iterators and shared memory and atomics for concurrent programming.

The evolution of JavaScript has been driven by the need to meet the demands of modern web development, including increased performance, scalability, and maintainability. As web applications have grown in complexity and sophistication, JavaScript has adapted to provide developers with the tools and capabilities needed to build robust and feature-rich applications.

In recent years, the JavaScript ecosystem has continued to expand, with the emergence of new tools, frameworks, and libraries. Node.js, a runtime environment for executing JavaScript code outside the browser, has become increasingly popular for server-side development, enabling developers to build full-stack JavaScript applications.

The rise of front-end frameworks like React, Vue.js, and Angular has further transformed the landscape of web development, offering developers powerful tools for building interactive and responsive user interfaces. These frameworks leverage the latest features of ECMAScript to provide developers with a modern and efficient development experience.

Looking ahead, the future of JavaScript appears promising, with ongoing efforts to improve the language and its ecosystem. Proposals for new features and enhancements are regularly discussed and standardized through the ECMAScript process, ensuring that JavaScript continues to evolve to meet the needs of developers and users alike. As the web continues to evolve, JavaScript will remain a critical technology, powering the next generation of web applications and experiences.

JavaScript, originating in the mid-1990s, is a pivotal language in web development, renowned for its versatility and wide-ranging applications. Its evolution, deeply intertwined with the growth of the internet, reflects the changing demands of web development. Initially developed by Brendan Eich at Netscape Communications Corporation, JavaScript was conceived as a client-side scripting language to enhance web pages with dynamic and interactive content. As the internet burgeoned, JavaScript's significance skyrocketed, becoming a fundamental pillar of modern web development.

In its nascent stage, JavaScript was rudimentary, mainly used for simple form validations and basic interactivity. Its syntax, reminiscent of C and Java, featured conventional constructs like variables, functions, loops, and conditionals. Despite its limitations, JavaScript showcased immense potential, driving innovation and experimentation in web development.

Over time, JavaScript underwent a metamorphosis, with successive iterations introducing groundbreaking features and enhancements. The release of ECMAScript 3 in 1999 marked a significant milestone, standardizing JavaScript and solidifying its core functionality. This version introduced essential concepts like regular expressions, exception handling, and array methods, laying the groundwork for future advancements.

In the early 2000s, ECMAScript 4 aimed to revolutionize JavaScript with ambitious features like classes, modules, and enhanced syntax. However, internal disputes within the ECMAScript committee and compatibility concerns thwarted its adoption, leading to its eventual abandonment. Despite this setback, JavaScript continued to evolve, with browser vendors introducing proprietary features and optimizations.

The year 2009 heralded a paradigm shift with the release of ECMAScript 5, a significant update that introduced essential features like strict mode, JSON support, and array methods such as **map()**, **filter()**, and **reduce()**. This version cemented JavaScript's status as a robust and capable language, fueling its widespread adoption across industries.

Subsequent iterations, notably ECMAScript 6 (ES6) released in 2015, revolutionized JavaScript development, introducing a plethora of groundbreaking features and syntactic enhancements. ES6 introduced arrow functions, template literals, destructuring assignment, and classes, among other modern constructs, vastly improving developer productivity and code expressiveness.

bashCopy code

Example of using Babel to transpile ES6 code to ES5 for compatibility babel script.js --out-file compiled.js

In this example, Babel is utilized to transpile an ES6 JavaScript file (**script.js**) into ES5 syntax, ensuring compatibility with older browsers and environments.

Furthermore, ES6 introduced modules, a standardized mechanism for organizing and encapsulating code, facilitating better code organization and reusability. Modules enabled developers to create modular, maintainable codebases, fostering collaboration and code sharing within the JavaScript community.

The evolution of JavaScript continued unabated, with subsequent ECMAScript versions introducing incremental improvements and new features. ES7 (2016) brought async/await, a powerful tool for writing asynchronous code in a synchronous style, simplifying asynchronous programming paradigms. ES8 (2017) introduced features like **Object.entries()**, **Object.values()**, and **String.padStart()**, enhancing JavaScript's utility and expressiveness.

In recent years, the ECMAScript specification adopted an annual release cycle, ensuring a steady stream of new features and enhancements. ESNext, the term coined for the upcoming ECMAScript versions, promises to deliver cutting-edge features like optional chaining, nullish coalescing, and private class fields, further solidifying JavaScript's position as a premier programming language.

bashCopy code

```
# Example of installing ECMAScript proposals using npm npm install proposal-name
```

In this example, npm is used to install an ECMAScript proposal (e.g., optional chaining) as a package, allowing developers to experiment with upcoming language features.

In summary, JavaScript's journey from its humble origins to its current prominence exemplifies the dynamic nature of web development. Its evolution, marked by successive iterations and groundbreaking features, mirrors the ever-changing landscape of the internet. As JavaScript continues to evolve, developers must stay abreast of new features and best practices, embracing innovation and pushing the boundaries of web development.

Chapter 2: Working with Variables and Data Types

Understanding variables and data types is foundational to mastering any programming language, including JavaScript. Variables serve as containers for storing data, allowing developers to manipulate and reference values within their programs. In JavaScript, variables are declared using the **var**, **let**, or **const** keywords, each with its own scope and behavior. The **var** keyword, introduced in earlier versions of JavaScript, declares variables with function scope, meaning they are accessible within the function in which they are defined. Conversely, the **let** and **const** keywords, introduced in ECMAScript 6 (ES6), declare variables with block scope, limiting their accessibility to the block in which they are declared. This distinction is crucial for understanding variable scoping and avoiding unintended side effects in JavaScript code.

bashCopy code

Example of declaring variables using var, let, and const in JavaScript var name = 'John'; let age = 30; const PI = 3.14;

In this example, variables **name**, **age**, and **PI** are declared using the **var**, **let**, and **const** keywords, respectively, each holding different types of data: a string, a number, and a constant value.

JavaScript supports various data types, including primitive types like strings, numbers, booleans, null, undefined, and symbols, as well as complex types like objects and functions. Understanding these data types is essential for writing robust and efficient JavaScript code. Strings, for example, represent sequences of characters enclosed within single or double quotation marks, while numbers can be integers, floating-point numbers, or in scientific notation. Booleans represent logical values **true** or **false**, while null and undefined represent the absence of a value. Symbols, introduced in ES6, are unique and immutable data types often used as property keys in objects.

javascriptCopy code

```javascript
// Example of different data types in JavaScript
let name = 'Alice'; // string
let age = 25; // number
let isStudent = true; // boolean
let score = null; // null
let address; // undefined
let uniqueId = Symbol('id'); // symbol
console.log(typeof name); // Output: string
console.log(typeof age); // Output: number
console.log(typeof isStudent); // Output: boolean
console.log(typeof score); // Output: object
console.log(typeof address); // Output: undefined
console.log(typeof uniqueId); // Output: symbol
```

In this example, variables **name**, **age**, **isStudent**, **score**, **address**, and **uniqueId** demonstrate different data types in JavaScript, and the **typeof** operator is used to determine the type of each variable.

Furthermore, JavaScript objects are complex data types that store collections of key-value pairs, allowing developers to represent structured data in their programs. Objects can contain various data types, including strings, numbers, booleans, arrays, and even other objects or functions. Accessing and manipulating object properties is a fundamental aspect of JavaScript programming, achieved using dot notation or bracket notation.

javascriptCopy code

```
// Example of creating and accessing object properties in JavaScript let person = { firstName: 'John', lastName: 'Doe', age: 30, isStudent: false, address: { city: 'New York', country: 'USA' }, sayHello: function() { return 'Hello, ' + this.firstName + ' ' + this.lastName + '!'; } };
console.log(person.firstName); // Output: John
console.log(person['age']); // Output: 30
console.log(person.address.city); // Output: New York console.log(person.sayHello()); // Output: Hello, John Doe!
```

In this example, the **person** object contains various properties, including **firstName**, **lastName**, **age**,

isStudent, **address**, and **sayHello**, demonstrating how to create and access object properties using dot notation and bracket notation.

Understanding variables and data types is fundamental to writing effective JavaScript code, enabling developers to store, manipulate, and represent data within their programs. By mastering variables and data types, developers can leverage the full power and flexibility of JavaScript to build robust and efficient web applications.

Variable declarations and initialization are fundamental concepts in programming, serving as the building blocks for creating and manipulating data within a program. In JavaScript, variables can be declared and initialized using various keywords, such as **var**, **let**, and **const**, each with its own scope and behavior. The **var** keyword, traditionally used in JavaScript for variable declaration, has function-level scope, meaning variables declared with **var** are accessible within the function in which they are defined. However, **var** variables can also be accessed outside of their declaring function, leading to potential issues with variable hoisting and unintended global scope. To address these issues, ECMAScript 6 (ES6) introduced two new keywords for variable declaration: **let** and **const**. Unlike **var**, variables declared with **let** and **const** have block-level scope, meaning they are accessible only within the block in which they are defined. Additionally, variables declared with **const** are immutable, meaning their value cannot be reassigned once initialized.

bashCopy code

Example of declaring and initializing variables using var, let, and const in JavaScript var name = 'John'; let age = 30; const PI = 3.14;

In this example, variables **name**, **age**, and **PI** are declared and initialized using the **var**, **let**, and **const** keywords, respectively. The **var** keyword is used to declare a variable **name** and assign it the value **'John'**, while the **let** keyword is used to declare a variable **age** and assign it the value **30**. Lastly, the **const** keyword is used to declare a constant variable **PI** and assign it the value **3.14**. Once initialized, the values of these variables can be accessed and manipulated throughout the program.

Variable initialization involves assigning an initial value to a variable at the time of declaration. In JavaScript, variables can be initialized with primitive values, such as strings, numbers, booleans, null, and undefined, as well as complex values, such as objects and functions. Primitive values are immutable, meaning their value cannot be changed after initialization, while complex values are mutable, meaning their properties can be modified.

javascriptCopy code

```
// Example of variable initialization with primitive
and complex values in JavaScript let name =
'Alice'; // string let age = 25; // number let
isStudent = true; // boolean let score = null; //
null let address; // undefined let person = {
firstName: 'Bob', lastName: 'Smith' }; // object let
greet = function() { return 'Hello, world!'; }; //
function
```

In this example, variables **name**, **age**, **isStudent**, **score**, and **address** are initialized with primitive values, including a string, a number, a boolean, null, and undefined, respectively. Additionally, variables **person** and **greet** are initialized with complex values, including an object and a function, respectively. Once initialized, these variables can be used throughout the program to store and manipulate data as needed.

Variable initialization is an essential concept in programming, enabling developers to create and manage data within their programs effectively. By understanding the various keywords for variable declaration and initialization in JavaScript, developers can write more robust and maintainable code. Additionally, understanding the differences between primitive and complex values helps developers make informed decisions when initializing variables in their programs. Overall, variable declaration and initialization are foundational concepts in programming, essential for building functional and efficient software applications.

Chapter 3: Control Flow: Conditionals and Loops

Conditional statements are indispensable tools in programming, enabling developers to control the flow of their code based on different conditions. In JavaScript, conditional statements include **if, else if, else**, and **switch**, each serving distinct purposes in decision-making. The **if** statement is the most basic form of conditional statement, allowing developers to execute a block of code if a specified condition is true. For example, the following code snippet demonstrates the use of the **if** statement to check if a given number is positive:

javascriptCopy code

```
let number = 10; if (number > 0) {
console.log('The number is positive.'); }
```

In this example, if the value of the variable **number** is greater than **0**, the message "The number is positive." will be displayed.

The **else** statement can be used in conjunction with **if** to specify a block of code to execute if the condition is false. For instance, consider the following code snippet:

javascriptCopy code

```javascript
let number = -5; if (number > 0) {
console.log('The number is positive.'); } else {
console.log('The number is not positive.'); }
```

In this example, if the value of the variable **number** is greater than **0**, the message "The number is positive." will be displayed; otherwise, the message "The number is not positive." will be displayed.

Additionally, the **else if** statement allows developers to specify multiple conditions to check sequentially. This is useful when there are more than two possible outcomes based on different conditions. Here's an example:

javascriptCopy code

```javascript
let number = 0; if (number > 0) { console.log('The
number is positive.'); } else if (number < 0) {
console.log('The number is negative.'); } else {
console.log('The number is zero.'); }
```

In this example, if the value of the variable **number** is greater than **0**, the message "The number is positive." will be displayed. If it is less than **0**, the message "The number is negative." will be displayed. Otherwise, if none of the conditions are met, the message "The number is zero." will be displayed.

Another powerful conditional statement in JavaScript is the **switch** statement, which provides an efficient way to handle multiple conditions based on the value of an expression. The **switch** statement

evaluates an expression and executes the corresponding case statement. Here's an example:
javascriptCopy code

```
let day = 'Monday'; switch (day) { case 'Monday': console.log('Today is Monday.'); break; case 'Tuesday': console.log('Today is Tuesday.'); break; case 'Wednesday': console.log('Today is Wednesday.'); break; default: console.log('Unknown day.'); }
```

In this example, the value of the variable **day** is compared against different cases, and the corresponding message is displayed based on the value. If none of the cases match, the **default** case is executed.

Conditional statements are essential for controlling the flow of a program based on different conditions. They allow developers to write more dynamic and flexible code, enabling applications to respond appropriately to various scenarios. By mastering conditional statements like **if**, **else**, and **switch**, developers can create more robust and efficient JavaScript applications.

Looping constructs are essential components of programming languages, enabling developers to execute a block of code repeatedly until a specified condition is met. In JavaScript, three primary loop constructs are available: **for, while**, and **do-while**, each serving distinct purposes in controlling the flow of code execution. The **for** loop is commonly used when the number of iterations is known in advance or when iterating over arrays or other collections. It consists of three parts: initialization, condition, and increment. Here's an example of a **for** loop that iterates from 1 to 5:

javascriptCopy code

```javascript
for (let i = 1; i <= 5; i++) { console.log(i); }
```

In this example, the loop initializes the variable **i** to 1, checks if **i** is less than or equal to 5, executes the loop body (printing the value of **i**), and then increments **i** by 1 in each iteration.

The **while** loop, on the other hand, is suitable for situations where the number of iterations is not known in advance but is based on a specific condition. It evaluates the condition before executing the loop body, and if the condition is true, the loop body is executed. Here's an example of a **while** loop that prints numbers from 1 to 5:

javascriptCopy code

```javascript
let i = 1; while (i <= 5) { console.log(i); i++; }
```

In this example, the loop continues to execute as long as the condition **i <= 5** is true. The variable **i** is initialized outside the loop, and its value is incremented within the loop body.

The **do-while** loop is similar to the **while** loop, but it evaluates the condition after executing the loop body. This means that the loop body is executed at least once, even if the condition is initially false. Here's an example of a **do-while** loop that prints numbers from 1 to 5:

javascriptCopy code

```
let i = 1; do { console.log(i); i++; } while (i <= 5);
```

In this example, the loop body is executed once, printing the value of **i**, and then the condition **i <= 5** is evaluated. If the condition is true, the loop continues to execute; otherwise, it terminates.

Each loop construct has its advantages and use cases. The **for** loop is typically used for iterating over a known range of values or collections, while the **while** loop is more suitable for situations where the number of iterations is not known in advance. The **do-while** loop is useful when you want to execute the loop body at least once before checking the condition.

Understanding and mastering these loop constructs is essential for writing efficient and readable JavaScript code. By choosing the appropriate loop construct for a given task and understanding how to control the flow of execution, developers can write more expressive and maintainable code. Whether it's iterating over arrays, processing user input, or implementing complex algorithms, loops are a fundamental tool in every developer's toolbox.

Chapter 4: Functions and Scope

In JavaScript, functions are crucial building blocks of any application, allowing developers to encapsulate reusable pieces of code and organize their programs more effectively. When it comes to defining functions, there are two primary approaches: function declarations and function expressions. Function declarations are defined using the **function** keyword followed by the function name and its parameters, if any. They are hoisted to the top of their scope, meaning they can be invoked before they are declared in the code. Here's an example of a function declaration:

javascriptCopy code

```
function greet(name) { return 'Hello, ' + name + '!'; }
```

In this example, the **greet** function is declared with a single parameter **name**, which is used to greet the specified person.

Function expressions, on the other hand, involve defining a function as part of an expression, typically by assigning it to a variable. Unlike function declarations, function expressions are not hoisted, meaning they cannot be invoked before they are defined. Here's an example of a function expression:

javascriptCopy code

```
const greet = function(name) { return 'Hello, ' + name + '!'; };
```

In this example, the **greet** function is assigned to the variable **greet** using a function expression syntax. It behaves similarly to the function declaration example, but the function is assigned to a variable instead.

Both function declarations and function expressions have their advantages and use cases. Function declarations are useful when you need to define a function that should be accessible throughout the scope, as they are hoisted to the top of their scope. This makes them suitable for defining utility functions or functions that are used in multiple places within a file or module.

Function expressions, on the other hand, offer more flexibility and can be assigned to variables dynamically. They are often used when you need to define functions dynamically, pass functions as arguments to other functions, or create functions conditionally based on certain criteria.

Here's an example demonstrating the use of a function expression as an argument to the **setTimeout** function:

javascriptCopy code

```
setTimeout(function() { console.log('Delayed message'); }, 1000);
```

In this example, a function expression is passed as the first argument to **setTimeout**, allowing the specified function to be executed after a delay of 1000 milliseconds.

Additionally, function expressions are commonly used when working with higher-order functions such as **map**, **filter**, and **reduce**, which expect a function as an argument.

Overall, both function declarations and function expressions are essential tools in JavaScript for defining functions. Understanding the differences between them and knowing when to use each approach is crucial for writing clean, readable, and maintainable code. Whether it's defining utility functions, creating callbacks, or working with higher-order functions, mastering function declarations and expressions is fundamental for any JavaScript developer.

Scope and closures are fundamental concepts in JavaScript that govern how variables and functions are accessed and manipulated within a program. Understanding these concepts is crucial for writing efficient and bug-free code.

Scope refers to the visibility and accessibility of variables and functions within a program. JavaScript has function scope, meaning variables defined within a function are only accessible within that

function or nested functions. This concept is demonstrated in the following example:
javascriptCopy code
function outerFunction() { var outerVariable = 'I am outer'; function innerFunction() { var innerVariable = 'I am inner'; console.log(outerVariable); // Accessible } console.log(innerVariable); // Error: innerVariable is not defined }

In this example, **outerVariable** is accessible within both **outerFunction** and **innerFunction**, while **innerVariable** is only accessible within **innerFunction**. This is because of the scope chain, which allows inner functions to access variables declared in their outer functions.

Closures, on the other hand, are a mechanism in JavaScript that allows functions to retain access to variables from their containing scope even after the outer function has finished executing. This is achieved by creating a closure, which bundles the function along with its lexical environment, including any variables it needs access to. Consider the following example:
javascriptCopy code
function createCounter() { var count = 0; return function() { return ++count; }; } var counter =

createCounter();   console.log(counter());   // Output: 1 console.log(counter()); // Output: 2

In this example, the **createCounter** function returns a new function that increments a **count** variable each time it's called. Even though **createCounter** has finished executing, the returned function still retains access to the **count** variable due to closures.

Understanding scope and closures is crucial for avoiding common pitfalls and writing more robust and maintainable code. When variables are not properly scoped, it can lead to unintended consequences and bugs in the code. Additionally, closures are commonly used in JavaScript for creating private variables, memoization, and implementing modules.

One common use case for closures is in event handling. Consider the following example:

javascriptCopy code

```
function handleClick() { var count = 0; return function() { console.log('Button clicked ' + (++count) + ' times'); }; } var button = document.getElementById('myButton');
button.addEventListener('click', handleClick());
```

In this example, every time the button is clicked, the count is incremented and logged to the console. The **handleClick** function returns a closure that retains access to the **count** variable, allowing it to maintain state across multiple invocations.

Understanding scope and closures is essential for writing efficient and bug-free JavaScript code. By mastering these concepts, developers can leverage the full power of JavaScript and build more reliable and maintainable applications. Whether it's understanding variable visibility, managing function scope, or harnessing the power of closures, a solid grasp of scope and closures is indispensable for JavaScript developers.

Chapter 5: Arrays and Objects: Complex Data Structures

Arrays are a fundamental data structure in JavaScript, providing a versatile way to store and manipulate collections of data. Understanding how to work with arrays efficiently is essential for writing effective JavaScript code.

One of the most basic operations when working with arrays is creating and initializing them. Arrays in JavaScript can be created using square brackets [ ] and can hold any combination of values, including numbers, strings, objects, or even other arrays. Here's an example of creating an array:

javascriptCopy code

const numbers = [1, 2, 3, 4, 5]; const fruits = ['apple', 'banana', 'orange']; const mixed = [1, 'two', { key: 'value' }];

Once an array is created, there are numerous methods and operations available to manipulate its contents. One common operation is accessing individual elements within the array. This can be done using square bracket notation with the index of the element, where the index starts at 0. For example:

javascriptCopy code

```javascript
const numbers = [1, 2, 3, 4, 5];
console.log(numbers[0]);    // Output: 1
console.log(numbers[2]); // Output: 3
```

Arrays also come with a variety of built-in methods for adding, removing, and modifying elements. One such method is **push()**, which adds one or more elements to the end of an array:

javascriptCopy code

```javascript
const fruits = ['apple', 'banana', 'orange'];
fruits.push('grape'); console.log(fruits); // Output:
['apple', 'banana', 'orange', 'grape']
```

Conversely, the **pop()** method removes the last element from an array:

javascriptCopy code

```javascript
const fruits = ['apple', 'banana', 'orange'];
fruits.pop(); console.log(fruits); // Output:
['apple', 'banana']
```

Another common operation is iterating over the elements of an array. This can be done using loops such as **for** loops or array iteration methods like **forEach()**. For example:

javascriptCopy code

```javascript
const numbers = [1, 2, 3, 4, 5]; for (let i = 0; i <
numbers.length; i++) { console.log(numbers[i]); }
// Output: // 1 // 2 // 3 // 4 // 5
```

Alternatively, using the **forEach()** method:

javascriptCopy code

```
const    numbers    =    [1,    2,    3,    4,    5];
numbers.forEach(function(number)                    {
console.log(number); }); // Output: // 1 // 2 // 3
// 4 // 5
```

JavaScript also provides array methods for filtering, mapping, and reducing arrays. The **filter()** method, for instance, creates a new array with all elements that pass a test implemented by the provided function:

javascriptCopy code

```
const    numbers    =    [1,    2,    3,    4,    5];    const
evenNumbers = numbers.filter(function(number)
{    return    number    %    2    ===    0;    });
console.log(evenNumbers); // Output: [2, 4]
```

Similarly, the **map()** method creates a new array by applying a function to each element of the original array:

javascriptCopy code

```
const numbers = [1, 2, 3, 4, 5]; const doubled =
numbers.map(function(number) { return number
* 2; }); console.log(doubled); // Output: [2, 4, 6, 8,
10]
```

Lastly, the **reduce()** method reduces an array to a single value by applying a function to each element and accumulating the result:

javascriptCopy code

```javascript
const numbers = [1, 2, 3, 4, 5]; const sum =
numbers.reduce(function(accumulator,
currentValue) { return accumulator + currentValue;
}, 0); console.log(sum); // Output: 15
```

These are just a few examples of the many methods and operations available for working with arrays in JavaScript. By mastering these techniques, developers can efficiently manipulate data structures and build powerful applications. Whether it's adding and removing elements, iterating over arrays, or performing complex transformations, arrays are a versatile tool in the JavaScript developer's toolkit.

JavaScript objects are versatile data structures used to store and manipulate complex data. Understanding how to work with objects effectively is essential for JavaScript developers. Objects in JavaScript consist of key-value pairs, where each key is a string (or symbol) and each value can be any data type, including other objects, functions, arrays, or primitive values like strings and numbers.

To create an object in JavaScript, you can use object literal notation, which involves enclosing key-value pairs within curly braces {}. For example:

javascriptCopy code

```javascript
const person = { name: 'John Doe', age: 30,
email: 'john@example.com', address: { street:
```

'123 Main St', city: 'Anytown', country: 'USA' },
sayHello: function() { console.log('Hello!'); } };

In this example, **person** is an object with properties such as **name**, **age**, **email**, and **address**. The **address** property is itself an object with nested properties. Additionally, the **sayHello** property is a method—a function assigned to a property.

Accessing properties of an object can be done using dot notation (**object.property**) or bracket notation (**object['property']**). For example:

javascriptCopy code

```
console.log(person.name); // Output: John Doe
console.log(person['age']); // Output: 30
```

Objects in JavaScript can be modified dynamically by adding, updating, or deleting properties. To add a new property to an object, simply assign a value to a new key:

javascriptCopy code

```
person.gender = 'Male';
```

To update an existing property, simply reassign its value:

javascriptCopy code

```
person.age = 31;
```

To delete a property from an object, you can use the **delete** keyword:

javascriptCopy code

```
delete person.email;
```

JavaScript objects also have built-in methods for working with properties. One such method is **Object.keys()**, which returns an array of a given object's own enumerable property names:
javascriptCopy code

```
const keys = Object.keys(person);
console.log(keys); // Output: ['name', 'age', 'address', 'sayHello']
```

Another useful method is **Object.values()**, which returns an array of a given object's own enumerable property values:
javascriptCopy code

```
const values = Object.values(person);
console.log(values); // Output: ['John Doe', 31, { street: '123 Main St', city: 'Anytown', country: 'USA' }, [Function: sayHello]]
```

Objects in JavaScript are often used in conjunction with arrays to represent more complex data structures. For example, an array of objects can be used to store a collection of similar entities, such as a list of users or products.

Furthermore, objects can have methods, which are functions defined as properties of an object. These methods can perform operations on the object's data or interact with other parts of the program.

Understanding JavaScript objects and how to work with their properties and methods is essential for building robust and maintainable JavaScript applications. By mastering these concepts, developers can leverage the full power of JavaScript's object-oriented capabilities to create dynamic and interactive web experiences.

Chapter 6: DOM Manipulation: Interacting with HTML

The Document Object Model, commonly referred to as the DOM, is a programming interface for web documents. It represents the structure of HTML and XML documents as a tree-like structure where each node represents an element, attribute, or piece of text within the document. The DOM provides a way for programs to manipulate the structure, style, and content of web pages dynamically.

To understand the DOM, it's essential to grasp its tree-like structure. At the top of the tree is the document node, which represents the entire HTML document. Beneath the document node are various types of nodes, including element nodes, text nodes, attribute nodes, and comment nodes. Element nodes represent HTML elements such as **<div>, <p>, <h1>**, and so on. Text nodes contain the text content of elements, while attribute nodes represent attributes of elements.

One of the fundamental features of the DOM is its ability to allow developers to access and manipulate elements on a web page using scripting languages such as JavaScript. This is done through a set of APIs provided by web browsers. For example, to access an element with a specific ID using JavaScript, you can use the **getElementById()** method:

javascriptCopy code

```
const element =
document.getElementById('myElement');
```

This command selects the HTML element with the ID **myElement** and assigns it to the variable **element**, allowing you to manipulate its properties, attributes, and contents programmatically.

Another commonly used method is **querySelector()**, which allows you to select elements using CSS-style selectors:

javascriptCopy code

```
const element =
document.querySelector('.myClass');
```

This command selects the first element with the class **myClass** and assigns it to the variable **element**. You can then modify its attributes, styles, or content using JavaScript.

Once you have selected an element, you can manipulate its properties, attributes, and content using the DOM API. For example, to change the text content of an element, you can use the **textContent** property:

javascriptCopy code

```
element.textContent = 'New content';
```

Similarly, to modify the value of an attribute, you can use the **setAttribute()** method:

javascriptCopy code

```
element.setAttribute('src', 'newImage.jpg');
```

These are just a few examples of the many methods and properties available in the DOM API for manipulating web documents dynamically.

In addition to manipulation, the DOM also allows developers to respond to user interactions and events. Event listeners can be attached to elements to execute code in response to events such as clicks, mouse movements, or keyboard inputs. For example, to execute a function when a button is clicked, you can use the **addEventListener()** method:

javascriptCopy code

```
element.addEventListener('click', function() { // Code to execute when the button is clicked });
```

This allows you to create interactive and dynamic web applications by responding to user actions in real-time.

Furthermore, the DOM facilitates the creation of dynamic and interactive web applications by enabling the creation and manipulation of HTML elements on the fly. This is particularly useful for applications that involve dynamically adding or removing content based on user actions or data from external sources.

Overall, the Document Object Model plays a crucial role in web development by providing a standardized interface for accessing, manipulating, and interacting with web documents. Understanding how to leverage the DOM effectively is essential for building modern web applications that are dynamic, interactive, and responsive to user input.

Manipulating DOM (Document Object Model) elements with JavaScript is a fundamental aspect of web development, allowing developers to dynamically change the content, structure, and style of web pages in response to user interactions, data updates, or other events. JavaScript provides a powerful set of APIs for accessing and modifying DOM elements directly from within a web page or web application.

One of the most common tasks when working with the DOM is selecting elements to manipulate. JavaScript provides several methods for selecting elements based on various criteria, such as their ID, class, tag name, or relationship to other elements. The **document.getElementById()** method, for example, allows you to select an element by its unique ID:

javascriptCopy code

```
const element = document.getElementById('myElement');
```

Similarly, the **document.querySelector()** method enables you to select elements using CSS-style selectors:

javascriptCopy code

```
const element = document.querySelector('.myClass');
```

Once you've selected an element, you can manipulate its properties, attributes, and content using JavaScript. For example, you can change the text content of an element using the **textContent** property:

javascriptCopy code

```
element.textContent = 'New content';
```

Or you can modify the value of an attribute using the **setAttribute()** method:

javascriptCopy code

```
element.setAttribute('src', 'newImage.jpg');
```

In addition to modifying existing elements, JavaScript also allows you to create new elements dynamically and append them to the DOM. This is particularly useful for building user interfaces or displaying data fetched from an external source. The **document.createElement()** method creates a new element with the specified tag name:

javascriptCopy code

```
const newElement = document.createElement('div');
```

You can then customize the newly created element by setting its properties or attributes before appending it to the DOM using methods like **appendChild()** or **insertBefore()**:

javascriptCopy code

```
parentElement.appendChild(newElement);
```

JavaScript also provides methods for removing elements from the DOM, such as **removeChild()**:

javascriptCopy code

```
parentElement.removeChild(childElement);
```

In addition to manipulating individual elements, JavaScript allows you to work with collections of elements using methods like **querySelectorAll()**, which returns a NodeList containing all elements that match a specified CSS selector:

javascriptCopy code

```
const elements = document.querySelectorAll('.myClass');
```

You can then iterate over the NodeList and perform operations on each element individually.

Another powerful feature of JavaScript is its ability to respond to user interactions and events by attaching event listeners to DOM elements. Event listeners allow you to execute code in response to events such as clicks, mouse movements, or keyboard inputs. You can attach event listeners using methods like **addEventListener()**:

javascriptCopy code

```
element.addEventListener('click', function() { //
```
Code to execute when the element is clicked });

This allows you to create interactive and responsive user interfaces that react to user actions in real-time.

Overall, manipulating DOM elements with JavaScript is a fundamental skill for web developers, enabling them to create dynamic, interactive, and responsive web applications. By leveraging JavaScript's powerful APIs for DOM manipulation, developers can create rich and engaging user experiences that enhance the usability and functionality of their websites and web applications.

Chapter 7: Events and Event Handling

Understanding JavaScript events is crucial for building interactive and dynamic web applications. Events are actions or occurrences that happen in the browser, such as a mouse click, keyboard press, or page load, which can trigger JavaScript functions to execute specific tasks or respond to user interactions.

To understand events, it's essential to grasp the concept of event-driven programming, where the flow of the program is determined by events rather than by a sequential execution of code. In event-driven programming, you define event handlers, which are functions that are executed when a specific event occurs. These event handlers are then attached to DOM elements using event listeners.

Event listeners are functions that listen for a particular event to occur on a specific DOM element and then execute a specified function in response. They are added to DOM elements using the **addEventListener()** method. For example, to listen for a click event on a button element and execute a function when the click event occurs, you can use the following code:

javascriptCopy code

```javascript
const            button            =
document.getElementById('myButton');
button.addEventListener('click', function() { //
Code to execute when the button is clicked });
```

JavaScript supports a wide range of events, categorized into different types such as mouse events, keyboard events, form events, and document events. Mouse events include events like click, mouseover, mouseout, and mousemove, which are triggered by mouse actions. Keyboard events, such as keydown, keyup, and keypress, are triggered by keyboard input. Form events, like submit, change, and focus, are related to form interactions. Document events, such as load and DOMContentLoaded, are related to the loading and manipulation of the DOM itself.

Understanding event propagation is also essential when working with JavaScript events. Event propagation refers to the process by which events propagate or "bubble" through the DOM tree from the target element to the root element. There are two phases of event propagation: capturing phase and bubbling phase. During the capturing phase, events are captured from the root element down to the target element. During the bubbling phase, events bubble up from the target element to the root element. You can control the event propagation behavior using the **addEventListener()**

method's third parameter, which specifies whether to use event capturing (true) or event bubbling (false).

In addition to standard DOM events, JavaScript also supports custom events, which are events that are created and dispatched programmatically rather than being triggered by user interactions. Custom events allow you to define and trigger your own events in response to specific conditions or actions within your application.

To dispatch a custom event, you can use the **CustomEvent** constructor to create a new custom event object and then dispatch it on a specific DOM element using the **dispatchEvent()** method. For example, to dispatch a custom event named "myEvent" on a button element, you can use the following code:

javascriptCopy code

```
const button = document.getElementById('myButton'); const event = new CustomEvent('myEvent', { detail: { key: 'value' } }); button.dispatchEvent(event);
```

Overall, understanding JavaScript events is essential for creating dynamic and interactive web applications. By leveraging events and event-driven programming, you can build applications that respond to user interactions in real-time, providing a rich and engaging user experience.

Handling events in web development is a fundamental aspect of creating dynamic and interactive user experiences. Events are actions or occurrences that happen in the browser, such as a mouse click, keyboard press, or page load, and handling these events allows developers to respond to user interactions in meaningful ways.

One common approach to handling events is through event listeners and event handlers. Event listeners are functions that are attached to DOM elements and wait for a specific event to occur, while event handlers are functions that execute in response to those events.

To add an event listener to a DOM element in JavaScript, you can use the **addEventListener()** method. This method takes two arguments: the type of event to listen for (such as "click" or "mouseover") and the function that should be executed when the event occurs. For example, to add a click event listener to a button element with the ID "myButton", you would use the following code:

```javascript
javascriptCopy code
const button = document.getElementById('myButton');
button.addEventListener('click', function() { // Code to execute when the button is clicked });
```

Event listeners provide a flexible way to handle events because you can attach multiple event listeners to the same element, allowing different functions to respond to the same event. Additionally, event listeners can be added and removed dynamically during runtime, enabling dynamic behavior in web applications.

Event handlers, on the other hand, are functions that are directly assigned to event attributes in HTML or through the **on** prefix in JavaScript. While event listeners provide a more modern and flexible approach to handling events, event handlers are still commonly used, especially in simpler applications or when working with older codebases.

In HTML, event handlers can be assigned directly to HTML elements using attributes such as **onclick**, **onmouseover**, **onkeyup**, etc. For example, to execute a function named **handleClick** when a button is clicked, you can use the following code:

htmlCopy code

```
<button onclick="handleClick()">Click me</button>
```

In JavaScript, event handlers can be assigned using the **on** prefix followed by the event type as a property of the DOM element. For example, to assign a function named **handleClick** as the click event handler for a button element, you can use the following code:

javascriptCopy code

```
const              button              =
document.getElementById('myButton');
button.onclick = handleClick;
```

It's important to note that event handlers assigned in this way can only have one function assigned to them at a time, and they overwrite any previously assigned event handlers for the same event type.

When working with event handlers and event listeners, it's essential to consider best practices for organizing and managing event handling code. This includes separating concerns, using descriptive function names, and avoiding inline event handlers whenever possible to improve code readability and maintainability.

Overall, event listeners and event handlers are powerful tools in web development for creating interactive and dynamic user experiences. By understanding how to use them effectively, developers can build applications that respond to user interactions in intuitive and engaging ways, enhancing the overall user experience.

Chapter 8: Asynchronous JavaScript: Promises and Callbacks

Asynchronous programming is a crucial concept in modern web development, allowing developers to execute multiple tasks concurrently without blocking the main execution thread. This approach is essential for handling time-consuming operations, such as fetching data from external sources, performing I/O operations, or executing complex computations, without slowing down the user interface or other parts of the application.

At its core, asynchronous programming involves executing tasks concurrently and handling their results once they become available. In traditional synchronous programming, tasks are executed sequentially, one after another, which can lead to performance bottlenecks, especially in applications that rely heavily on network requests or disk operations.

In JavaScript, asynchronous programming is commonly achieved using asynchronous functions, callbacks, promises, and more recently, async/await syntax. These techniques allow developers to write non-blocking code that can perform tasks in the background while the main execution thread continues to run other code.

One of the most common patterns for asynchronous programming in JavaScript is the use of callback functions. Callbacks are functions that are passed as arguments to other functions and are executed once the asynchronous operation is complete. For example, the **setTimeout()** function in JavaScript takes a callback function as its first argument and executes it after a specified delay:

javascriptCopy code

```javascript
setTimeout(() => { console.log('This code runs after 1 second.'); }, 1000);
```

While callback functions are effective for handling asynchronous operations, they can lead to callback hell, a situation where nested callbacks become difficult to manage and understand, resulting in code that is hard to read and maintain.

To address this issue, JavaScript introduced promises, which provide a cleaner and more structured way to handle asynchronous operations. Promises represent the eventual completion or failure of an asynchronous operation and allow developers to chain multiple asynchronous operations together in a more readable and manageable way.

Here's an example of using promises to handle asynchronous code:

javascriptCopy code

```
const fetchData = () => { return new
Promise((resolve, reject) => { // Simulate fetching
data from an API setTimeout(() => { const data = {
message: 'Data fetched successfully' };
resolve(data); }, 1000); }); }; fetchData()
.then((data) => { console.log(data); })
.catch((error) => { console.error('Error fetching
data:', error); });
```

In this example, the **fetchData()** function returns a promise that resolves with the fetched data after a delay. We can then use the **.then()** method to handle the successful completion of the promise and the **.catch()** method to handle any errors that occur during the asynchronous operation.

While promises provide a significant improvement over callback-based asynchronous code, they can still result in nested chains of **.then()** methods, especially when dealing with multiple asynchronous operations.

To address this limitation and further simplify asynchronous code, JavaScript introduced async/await syntax, which allows developers to write asynchronous code in a more synchronous-looking style. With async/await, developers can write code that looks and behaves like synchronous code, while still benefiting from the non-blocking nature of asynchronous programming.

Here's how you can rewrite the previous example using async/await:

javascriptCopy code

```
const fetchData = () => { return new Promise((resolve, reject) => { // Simulate fetching data from an API setTimeout(() => { const data = { message: 'Data fetched successfully' }; resolve(data); }, 1000); }); }; const fetchDataAsync = async () => { try { const data = await fetchData(); console.log(data); } catch (error) { console.error('Error fetching data:', error); } }; fetchDataAsync();
```

In this example, the **fetchDataAsync()** function is marked as **async**, which allows us to use the **await** keyword inside the function to pause execution until the promise returned by **fetchData()** is resolved. This makes the code easier to read and understand compared to the promise-based version.

Asynchronous programming is a fundamental concept in modern web development, and mastering it is essential for building efficient, responsive, and scalable web applications. By understanding the principles of asynchronous programming and how to use techniques like callbacks, promises, and async/await, developers can write code that performs well under various conditions and provides a seamless user experience.

Asynchronous programming is a fundamental concept in modern web development, allowing tasks to be executed independently of the main program flow. This is particularly crucial when dealing with time-consuming operations such as network requests, file system operations, or database queries. JavaScript, as a single-threaded language, handles asynchronous operations through event loops, callbacks, promises, and more recently, async/await syntax.

Callbacks are a traditional approach to handle asynchronous operations in JavaScript. They are functions passed as arguments to another function, which is then invoked once the asynchronous task completes. Callbacks provide a way to execute code after a task finishes without blocking the main thread. For instance, consider the following example of handling a file read operation using callbacks:

javascriptCopy code

```
const fs = require('fs'); fs.readFile('example.txt', 'utf8', (err, data) => { if (err) { console.error('Error reading file:', err); return; } console.log('File content:', data); });
```

In this code snippet, the **readFile** function asynchronously reads the contents of a file. Once the operation completes, the callback function is invoked, either with an error or the file data.

While callbacks serve their purpose, they can lead to callback hell or pyramid of doom when multiple asynchronous operations are nested. This can make the code hard to read and maintain. Promises were introduced to mitigate this issue by providing a cleaner and more structured way to handle asynchronous operations.

Promises represent a value that may be available now, in the future, or never. They have three states: pending, fulfilled, or rejected. Promises allow chaining of asynchronous operations using **.then()** and **.catch()** methods, which makes the code more readable and manageable. Here's how the previous file reading example looks using promises:

javascriptCopy code

```
const fs = require('fs').promises;
fs.readFile('example.txt', 'utf8').then(data => {
console.log('File content:', data); }).catch(err => {
console.error('Error reading file:', err); });
```

In this example, **readFile** returns a promise that resolves with the file data when successful or rejects with an error if something goes wrong.

Promises provide a cleaner way to handle asynchronous operations, but they still require nesting when dealing with multiple asynchronous tasks. To address this, async/await was introduced in ES2017, offering a more synchronous-looking syntax for handling asynchronous code.

Async functions allow you to write asynchronous code as if it were synchronous, making it easier to understand and maintain. The **async** keyword is used to declare an asynchronous function, and the **await** keyword is used to pause the execution of an async function until a promise is settled. Here's how the previous example looks with async/await:

javascriptCopy code

```
const fs = require('fs').promises; async function readFileAsync() { try { const data = await fs.readFile('example.txt', 'utf8'); console.log('File content:', data); } catch (err) { console.error('Error reading file:', err); } } readFileAsync();
```

In this code, the **readFileAsync** function is declared as asynchronous using the **async** keyword, and the **await** keyword is used to wait for the **readFile** promise to settle before proceeding.

Async/await syntax offers a more readable and maintainable way to write asynchronous code, especially when dealing with multiple asynchronous operations or complex control flows.

In summary, asynchronous programming is essential for handling time-consuming tasks in JavaScript. Callbacks, promises, and async/await are different techniques for managing asynchronous code, each with its advantages and use cases. Understanding these concepts is crucial for writing efficient and maintainable JavaScript code.

Chapter 9: AJAX and Fetch API: Making HTTP Requests

AJAX (Asynchronous JavaScript and XML) plays a crucial role in modern web development by enabling asynchronous communication between a web browser and a server, allowing for dynamic and interactive user experiences without requiring a full page reload. Understanding AJAX and its underlying principles is essential for web developers to create responsive and efficient web applications.

At its core, AJAX is a set of techniques used to send and receive data from a web server asynchronously, typically using the XMLHttpRequest (XHR) object in JavaScript. This allows web pages to update content dynamically without requiring the entire page to reload. Instead, only specific portions of the page are updated, resulting in a smoother and more responsive user experience.

To demonstrate the basics of AJAX, let's consider a simple example of fetching data from a server and updating a webpage without reloading the entire page. Suppose we have an HTML file with a button and a div element to display the fetched data:

htmlCopy code

```
<!DOCTYPE html> <html lang="en"> <head>
<meta charset="UTF-8"> <meta name="viewport"
```

content="width=device-width, initial-scale=1.0">
<title>AJAX Example</title> </head> <body>
<button onclick="loadData()">Load Data</button>
<div id="data"></div> <script> function loadData() {
// Create a new XMLHttpRequest object var xhr =
new XMLHttpRequest(); // Configure the request
xhr.open('GET', 'data.json', true); // Set up event
handler for when the request completes xhr.onload
= function() { if (xhr.status >= 200 && xhr.status <
300) { // Update the div element with the fetched
data document.getElementById('data').innerHTML =
xhr.responseText; } else { console.error('Request
failed with status:', xhr.status); } }; // Send the
request xhr.send(); } </script> </body> </html>

In this example, when the "Load Data" button is
clicked, the **loadData** function is called, which
creates a new XMLHttpRequest object. The **open**
method is used to configure the request, specifying
the HTTP method (GET), URL ('data.json' in this
case), and whether the request should be
asynchronous (true).

The **onload** event handler is set to handle the
response when the request completes successfully.
Inside the event handler, we check if the status
code of the response is in the success range (200-
299), and if so, we update the content of the div
element with the response text using the
innerHTML property.

Finally, the request is sent using the **send** method. When the request completes, the **onload** event handler is triggered, and the data returned from the server is displayed on the webpage without requiring a full page reload.

AJAX is commonly used in web development for various purposes, such as fetching data from a server, submitting form data asynchronously, and updating content dynamically based on user actions. It enables developers to create more interactive and responsive web applications, leading to a better user experience.

In addition to XMLHttpRequest, modern web development often utilizes the Fetch API, which provides a more modern and flexible interface for making network requests. The Fetch API offers a promise-based approach, making it easier to handle asynchronous operations and work with data in a more concise and readable manner.

javascriptCopy code

```
fetch('data.json') .then(response => { if
(!response.ok) { throw new Error('Network
response was not ok'); } return response.json(); })
.then(data => { // Update the div element with the
fetched                                    data
document.getElementById('data').innerHTML    =
JSON.stringify(data);  })  .catch(error  =>  {
```

```
console.error('There was a problem with the fetch
operation:', error.message); });
```
In this example, the Fetch API is used to fetch data from the 'data.json' URL. The **fetch** function returns a promise that resolves to the Response object representing the response to the request. We then use the **.json()** method to parse the response body as JSON.

The **.then()** method is used to handle the resolved promise and extract the JSON data from the response. If the request is successful, the data is updated on the webpage. If there is an error during the fetch operation, the **.catch()** method is used to handle the error and log an error message to the console.

Overall, AJAX and the Fetch API are powerful tools for building dynamic and interactive web applications. By understanding how to use these techniques effectively, developers can create more efficient and engaging user experiences on the web.

The Fetch API represents a modern approach to making HTTP requests in JavaScript, providing a more flexible and intuitive interface compared to traditional methods like XMLHttpRequest. Introduced as part of the ES6 specification, the Fetch API simplifies the process of fetching resources from a server and handling responses, making it a preferred choice for many developers when working with network requests.

To understand the Fetch API, let's explore its syntax and features through an example. Suppose we have a web application that needs to fetch data from a remote server and display it on the webpage. Here's how we can use the Fetch API to accomplish this task:

javascriptCopy code

```
fetch('https://api.example.com/data')
.then(response => { if (!response.ok) { throw new Error('Network response was not ok'); } return response.json(); }) .then(data => { // Process the fetched data console.log(data); }) .catch(error => { console.error('There was a problem with the fetch operation:', error.message); });
```

In this example, the **fetch** function is used to initiate a GET request to the specified URL ('https://api.example.com/data'). The **fetch** function returns a promise that resolves to a Response object representing the response to the request.

We then use the **.then()** method to handle the resolved promise and extract the JSON data from the response using the **.json()** method. If the request is successful (i.e., the response status is in the 200-299 range), the JSON data is processed further. If there is an error during the fetch operation, the **.catch()** method is used to handle the error and log an error message to the console.

One of the key advantages of the Fetch API is its simplicity and ease of use. The fetch function accepts a URL and an optional configuration object as parameters, allowing developers to customize the request by specifying options such as the HTTP method, headers, and request body.

For example, to send a POST request with JSON data, you can use the following syntax:

javascriptCopy code

```
fetch('https://api.example.com/data', { method:
'POST', headers: { 'Content-Type':
'application/json' }, body: JSON.stringify({ key1:
'value1', key2: 'value2' }) }) .then(response =>
response.json()) .then(data => { // Process the
response data  console.log(data); }) .catch(error =>
{ console.error('There was a problem with the
fetch operation:', error.message); });
```

In this example, we specify the HTTP method as 'POST' and set the Content-Type header to 'application/json' to indicate that we are sending JSON data in the request body. The JSON data is converted to a string using **JSON.stringify()** before being sent in the request.

The Fetch API also supports other HTTP methods such as PUT, DELETE, and PATCH, as well as options for configuring request headers, timeouts, and more. Additionally, it provides built-in support for handling different types of responses, including JSON, text, and binary data.

Overall, the Fetch API offers a modern and versatile solution for making HTTP requests in JavaScript, making it easier for developers to work with network resources and build dynamic web applications. Its intuitive syntax, promise-based approach, and support for modern features make it a valuable tool in the web developer's toolkit.

Chapter 10: Error Handling and Debugging Techniques

Identifying and handling JavaScript errors is a crucial aspect of web development, as errors can occur due to various reasons such as syntax mistakes, runtime issues, or unexpected behaviors in the code. Properly identifying and handling errors ensures that applications remain robust and user-friendly, providing a seamless experience for users.

One of the first steps in identifying errors is to understand the different types of errors that can occur in JavaScript code. These errors are categorized into three main types: syntax errors, runtime errors, and logic errors.

Syntax errors occur when the code violates the rules of the JavaScript language, such as misspelled keywords, missing parentheses, or incorrect variable names. These errors are detected by the JavaScript engine during the parsing phase and are typically displayed in the browser's console with a descriptive error message, making them relatively easy to identify and fix.

For example, if we have a syntax error in our code: javascriptCopy code

```
console.log('Hello, world!')
```

But mistakenly misspelled the **console** keyword as **consoel**:

javascriptCopy code

```
consoel.log('Hello, world!');
```

The browser's console would display a syntax error indicating that **consoel** is not defined, helping us identify the issue quickly.

Runtime errors, on the other hand, occur during the execution of the code and are often caused by unexpected conditions or invalid operations. These errors can manifest as exceptions, such as **TypeError**, **ReferenceError**, or **RangeError**, and may occur when trying to access properties of undefined variables, calling non-existent functions, or performing arithmetic operations on non-numeric values.

To handle runtime errors effectively, developers can use try-catch blocks to catch and gracefully handle exceptions that may occur during the execution of their code. Here's an example of using a try-catch block to handle a runtime error:

javascriptCopy code

```
try { // Attempt to access a property of an undefined                                         variable
console.log(undefinedVariable.property); } catch
(error) { // Handle the error gracefully
console.error('An        error        occurred:',
error.message); }
```

In this example, if **undefinedVariable** is not defined, a **ReferenceError** will occur when trying to access its property. However, the try-catch block allows us to catch the error and handle it without causing the entire application to crash.

Lastly, logic errors occur when the code does not produce the expected output due to incorrect implementation or flawed logic. These errors can be more challenging to identify and debug, as they may not result in immediate error messages or exceptions. Instead, they may cause the application to behave unexpectedly or produce incorrect results.

To identify and fix logic errors, developers can use various debugging techniques such as console logging, breakpoints, and code inspection tools. By systematically analyzing the code and tracing the flow of execution, developers can pinpoint the source of the error and make the necessary corrections to ensure the desired behavior.

In addition to understanding the types of errors, it's essential to implement error handling mechanisms that provide feedback to users and developers when errors occur. For user-facing applications, displaying informative error messages or providing fallback options can help users understand what went wrong and how to proceed. For developers, logging errors to the console or sending error reports to a server can assist in diagnosing and troubleshooting issues in production environments.

In summary, identifying and handling JavaScript errors is a critical aspect of web development that ensures the reliability and stability of applications. By understanding the types of errors, implementing proper error handling techniques, and using debugging tools effectively, developers can create robust and resilient applications that deliver a seamless user experience.

Debugging JavaScript code is an essential skill for developers to diagnose and fix issues in their applications efficiently. JavaScript, being a dynamic and loosely-typed language, can introduce various types of errors, including syntax errors, runtime errors, and logical errors. To address these errors effectively, developers rely on a combination of tools and techniques that allow them to inspect and debug their code thoroughly.

One of the most commonly used tools for debugging JavaScript code is the browser's built-in developer tools, which provide a suite of features for inspecting and debugging web applications. To access the developer tools in popular browsers like Google Chrome, Mozilla Firefox, or Microsoft Edge, developers can typically use the following keyboard shortcuts:

Google Chrome: **Ctrl + Shift + I** or **F12**

Mozilla Firefox: **Ctrl + Shift + I** or **F12**

Microsoft Edge: **Ctrl + Shift + I** or **F12**

Once the developer tools are open, developers can navigate to the "Console" tab to view any error messages or log output generated by their JavaScript code. The console also allows developers to execute JavaScript code directly and interact with the page's Document Object Model (DOM), making it a valuable tool for debugging.

In addition to the console, developer tools offer features such as breakpoints, which allow developers to pause the execution of their code at specific points and inspect the program's state. By setting breakpoints at critical junctures in their code, developers can step through their code line by line, examine variable values, and identify the source of errors more effectively.

Another useful feature of developer tools is the ability to inspect the DOM and CSS properties of elements on the page. This can be particularly helpful when debugging issues related to DOM manipulation or CSS styling, allowing developers to identify and resolve layout or styling issues quickly.

Apart from browser-based tools, developers can also use standalone debugging tools like Visual Studio Code or JetBrains WebStorm, which offer advanced debugging capabilities for JavaScript code. These tools provide features such as integrated debugging consoles, variable watchers, call stack inspection, and step-through debugging, enabling developers to debug their code more efficiently within their preferred development environment.

Furthermore, developers can leverage browser extensions and plugins to enhance their debugging workflow. For example, the "React Developer Tools" extension for Google Chrome provides additional debugging features specifically tailored for React applications, such as inspecting component hierarchies and viewing component state.

In addition to tools, developers employ various debugging techniques to troubleshoot issues in their JavaScript code effectively. One common technique is to use console logging to output variable values, function calls, or program flow at specific points in the code. By strategically placing console.log statements throughout their code, developers can gain insights into how their code is executing and identify potential issues.

Another technique is to use assertions and unit tests to verify the behavior of individual functions or modules within the codebase. By writing test cases that cover different scenarios and edge cases, developers can validate the correctness of their code and detect regressions or unexpected behavior early in the development process.

Moreover, developers can adopt a systematic approach to debugging, starting with a thorough analysis of the problem and gathering relevant information, such as error messages, stack traces, and user reports. Once the issue is identified, developers can use a combination of tools and techniques to isolate the root cause of the problem and implement a solution.

In summary, debugging JavaScript code is a critical skill for developers to ensure the reliability and functionality of their web applications. By leveraging a combination of tools such as browser developer tools, standalone debugging environments, and browser extensions, along with debugging techniques like console logging, assertions, and unit tests, developers can effectively diagnose and fix issues in their code, resulting in more robust and resilient applications.

Chapter 11: Advanced JavaScript Patterns and Best Practices

Design patterns in JavaScript play a crucial role in structuring and organizing code to address common software design problems. Among the various design patterns available, the Singleton, Module, and Factory patterns are widely used in JavaScript development to promote code reusability, maintainability, and scalability.

The Singleton pattern ensures that a class has only one instance and provides a global point of access to that instance. This pattern is particularly useful when there is a need to restrict the instantiation of a class to a single object, such as managing configuration settings, logging functionality, or database connections. To implement the Singleton pattern in JavaScript, developers can define a class with a private constructor and a static method to access the singleton instance. Here's an example of implementing the Singleton pattern:

javascriptCopy code

```
class    Singleton    {    constructor()    {    if
(!Singleton.instance) { Singleton.instance = this; }
return  Singleton.instance; } // Other methods and
properties    can    be    added    here    }    const
```

singletonInstance = new Singleton();
Object.freeze(singletonInstance); export default singletonInstance;

In this example, the Singleton class ensures that only one instance of itself is created and provides a static method to access that instance. By exporting the singleton instance and freezing it using **Object.freeze()**, developers prevent accidental modifications to the instance.

The Module pattern is another commonly used design pattern in JavaScript, providing a way to encapsulate and organize code into modular components. It promotes encapsulation by keeping the internal state of a module private and exposing a public interface for interacting with it. Modules help in reducing namespace pollution and preventing conflicts between different parts of the codebase. In JavaScript, modules can be implemented using the revealing module pattern, which leverages closures to create private variables and functions. Here's an example of implementing the Module pattern:

javascriptCopy code

```
const module = (function() { let privateVariable =
'This is private'; function privateFunction() { return
'This is also private'; } return { publicMethod:
function() { console.log(privateVariable);
console.log(privateFunction()); } }; })();
```

module.publicMethod(); // Output: "This is private" and "This is also private"

In this example, the module is defined as an immediately-invoked function expression (IIFE) that returns an object containing the public interface of the module. The privateVariable and privateFunction are inaccessible from outside the module, ensuring data encapsulation.

The Factory pattern is used to create objects without specifying the exact class of object that will be created. Instead of directly instantiating objects using a constructor function, developers use factory functions to encapsulate object creation logic and provide a common interface for creating different types of objects. This pattern promotes loose coupling between the client code and the objects being created, making it easier to extend and maintain the codebase. Here's an example of implementing the Factory pattern:

javascriptCopy code

```
class Product { constructor(name, price) {
this.name = name; this.price = price; } } class
ProductFactory { createProduct(type) { switch
(type) { case 'book': return new Product('Book',
10); case 'movie': return new Product('Movie',
20); default: throw new Error('Invalid product
type'); } } } const factory = new ProductFactory();
const book = factory.createProduct('book');
```

```
console.log(book); // Output: Product { name:
"Book", price: 10 }
```
In this example, the ProductFactory class encapsulates the logic for creating different types of products (e.g., books, movies) and provides a common interface (createProduct method) for creating them. Clients can use the factory to create product objects without needing to know the specific implementation details.

Overall, the Singleton, Module, and Factory patterns are powerful tools in the JavaScript developer's toolkit for structuring code, promoting encapsulation, and improving maintainability. By understanding and applying these design patterns effectively, developers can write cleaner, more modular, and easier-to-maintain JavaScript codebases.

Writing maintainable JavaScript code is essential for the long-term success of any project. Adopting best practices not only improves code readability and understandability but also facilitates collaboration among team members and reduces the likelihood of introducing bugs. In this section, we'll explore several JavaScript best practices that contribute to writing maintainable code.

1. Use Descriptive Variable Names

Choosing meaningful and descriptive variable names is crucial for code readability. Avoid single-letter variable names or cryptic abbreviations that may confuse other developers or even your future self. Use descriptive names that convey the purpose or content of the variable.

javascriptCopy code

```
// Bad let x = 10; // Good let itemCount = 10;
```

2. Follow Consistent Code Formatting

Consistent code formatting improves code readability and makes it easier to understand and maintain. Establish coding conventions within your team and use tools like ESLint or Prettier to enforce them automatically.

javascriptCopy code

```
// Inconsistent formatting function foo(){ let x= 10 ; return x +1; } // Consistent formatting function foo() { let x = 10; return x + 1; }
```

3. Use Strict Mode

Enabling strict mode (**'use strict';**) helps catch common coding mistakes and prevents certain actions that are considered bad practice. It encourages cleaner JavaScript code by disallowing the use of undeclared variables and deprecated features.

javascriptCopy code

```
'use strict'; // This will throw a ReferenceError in strict mode x = 10;
```

4. Avoid Global Variables

Global variables can lead to naming conflicts and unintended side effects. Minimize the use of global variables and prefer encapsulating variables and functions within modules or closures.

javascriptCopy code

```
// Bad: pollutes global namespace let counter = 0;
function incrementCounter() { counter++; } //
Good: encapsulated within a module const
counterModule = (function() { let counter = 0;
return { increment: function() { counter++; },
getCount: function() { return counter; } }; })();
```

5. Modularize Code

Break down your code into smaller, reusable modules. Modularization promotes code reusability, maintainability, and testability. Use ES6 modules or a module bundler like Webpack to organize your code into separate files.

javascriptCopy code

```
// MathUtils.js export function add(a, b) { return
a + b; } // main.js import { add } from
'./MathUtils.js'; console.log(add(3, 4)); // Output:
7
```

6. Avoid Nested Callbacks (Callback Hell)

Nested callbacks can lead to complex and hard-to-read code known as "callback hell." Use promises or async/await to handle asynchronous operations sequentially and improve code readability.

javascriptCopy code

```javascript
// Callback Hell getData(function(data) {
getMoreData(data, function(moreData) {
processMoreData(moreData, function(finalData) {
console.log(finalData); }); }); }); // Using Promises
getData()                          .then(getMoreData)
.then(processMoreData)          .then(console.log)
.catch(console.error);
```

7. Write Unit Tests

Unit tests help verify the correctness of your code and catch regressions when making changes. Adopt a testing framework like Jest or Mocha and write tests for critical parts of your codebase, including functions, modules, and components.

javascriptCopy code

```javascript
// Example test using Jest function add(a, b) {
return a + b; } test('adds 1 + 2 to equal 3', () => {
expect(add(1, 2)).toBe(3); });
```

8. Document Your Code

Add comments and documentation to explain the purpose, behavior, and usage of your code. Use JSDoc or similar tools to generate documentation from your code comments automatically.

javascriptCopy code

```javascript
/** * Calculates the sum of two numbers. *
@param {number} a - The first number. * @param
{number} b - The second number. * @returns
```

{number} The sum of the two numbers. */ function add(a, b) { return a + b; }

9. Regularly Refactor Your Code

Refactoring involves restructuring existing code to improve its readability, performance, and maintainability. Regularly review and refactor your codebase to eliminate duplication, improve naming, and simplify complex logic.

10. Follow Code Review Practices

Encourage peer code reviews within your team to catch bugs, share knowledge, and ensure adherence to coding standards and best practices. Use tools like GitHub's pull requests for collaborative code reviews.

By following these JavaScript best practices, you can write code that is easier to understand, maintain, and extend, ultimately leading to a more robust and reliable software application.

Chapter 12: Building Dynamic Web Applications: Real-World Projects

Building interactive web applications is one of the most practical and rewarding applications of JavaScript in modern web development. JavaScript, alongside HTML and CSS, forms the foundation for creating dynamic and engaging user experiences on the web. In this section, we'll explore various techniques and approaches for building interactive web applications using JavaScript.

1. DOM Manipulation

The Document Object Model (DOM) is a programming interface that represents the structure of HTML documents. JavaScript allows developers to manipulate the DOM dynamically, enabling the creation of interactive web pages. DOM manipulation involves accessing and modifying HTML elements, attributes, and styles in response to user actions or application events.

javascriptCopy code

```
// Example: Changing text content dynamically
const element = document.getElementById('myElement');
element.textContent = 'Hello, World!';
```

2. Event Handling

Event handling is a fundamental aspect of building interactive web applications. JavaScript enables developers to respond to user interactions such as clicks, keypresses, mouse movements, and form submissions. Event listeners are attached to HTML elements to execute specific actions when events occur.

javascriptCopy code

```
// Example: Adding a click event listener const button = document.getElementById('myButton'); button.addEventListener('click', function() { console.log('Button clicked!'); });
```

3. Form Validation

Form validation is essential for ensuring data integrity and user input correctness in web applications. JavaScript can be used to validate form fields in real-time, providing instant feedback to users about input errors or invalid data.

javascriptCopy code

```
// Example: Form validation using regular expressions const emailInput = document.getElementById('email'); const emailPattern = /^[^\s@]+@[^\s@]+\.[^\s@]+$/; emailInput.addEventListener('input', function() { if (!emailPattern.test(emailInput.value)) { emailInput.setCustomValidity('Invalid email
```

address'); } else { emailInput.setCustomValidity("");
} });

4. AJAX and Fetch API

Asynchronous JavaScript and XML (AJAX) enables web applications to communicate with servers asynchronously without reloading the entire page. The Fetch API provides a modern approach for making HTTP requests and handling responses in JavaScript.

javascriptCopy code

```
// Example: Fetching data from a REST API
fetch('https://api.example.com/data')
.then(response => response.json()) .then(data =>
{ console.log(data); }) .catch(error => {
console.error('Error fetching data:', error); });
```

5. Client-Side Routing

Client-side routing allows web applications to navigate between different views or pages without reloading the entire page from the server. JavaScript libraries like React Router or Vue Router facilitate client-side routing by managing application routes and rendering components based on URL changes.

javascriptCopy code

```
// Example: Setting up client-side routes with React
Router import { BrowserRouter as Router, Route,
Switch } from 'react-router-dom'; function App() {
```

```
return ( <Router> <Switch> <Route path="/" exact
component={Home} /> <Route path="/about"
component={About} /> <Route path="/contact"
component={Contact} /> </Switch> </Router> ); }
```

6. Animation and Effects

JavaScript enables the creation of interactive animations and visual effects to enhance user experience. Libraries like GSAP (GreenSock Animation Platform) or CSS transitions and animations can be used to animate elements on the web page dynamically.

javascriptCopy code

```
// Example: Animating an element with GSAP
gsap.to('.box', { duration: 1, x: 100, rotation: 360 });
```

7. Real-Time Data Updates

Web applications often require real-time data updates to display the latest information to users. JavaScript frameworks like Angular, React, or Vue.js, along with technologies like WebSockets or Server-Sent Events (SSE), enable real-time data synchronization between the client and server.

javascriptCopy code

```
// Example: Real-time data updates with
WebSocket const socket = new
WebSocket('wss://api.example.com/socket');
socket.onmessage = function(event) { const data
```

= JSON.parse(event.data); console.log('Received data:', data); };

8. Client-Side Storage

JavaScript provides various client-side storage mechanisms like Web Storage (localStorage and sessionStorage) and IndexedDB for storing data locally on the user's device. This allows web applications to persist user preferences, settings, or cached data.

javascriptCopy code

```
// Example: Storing data in localStorage
localStorage.setItem('username', 'john_doe');
const username = localStorage.getItem('username');
console.log('Username:', username);
```

By leveraging these techniques and practices, developers can create highly interactive and responsive web applications that deliver a seamless user experience. JavaScript's versatility and ubiquity make it an indispensable tool for building modern web applications with rich functionality and interactivity.

JavaScript is not only a fundamental language for web development but also a powerful tool for building real-world projects that solve practical problems and deliver value to users. In this section, we'll delve into several case studies that demonstrate how JavaScript can be applied to develop diverse and impactful applications.

1. E-commerce Platform

One common application of JavaScript is in building e-commerce platforms, which enable businesses to sell products or services online. JavaScript frameworks like React, Vue.js, or Angular are often used to create dynamic user interfaces for browsing products, adding items to the shopping cart, and completing transactions.

For instance, developers might use React along with libraries like Redux for state management and React Router for navigation to build a responsive and interactive e-commerce website. JavaScript is employed to handle user interactions, validate input data, and communicate with backend APIs for fetching product information and processing orders.

2. Social Media Dashboard

Another example is the development of a social media dashboard, which allows users to manage multiple social media accounts and monitor engagement metrics in one place. JavaScript frameworks like Angular or Vue.js are commonly utilized to create a single-page application (SPA) with real-time updates and responsive design.

JavaScript is employed to integrate with social media APIs such as Facebook Graph API or Twitter API to fetch user data, post updates, and track analytics. Additionally, libraries like Chart.js or D3.js are used to visualize data and display insights such as follower growth, engagement rates, and post performance.

3. Task Management Application

Task management applications help users organize their tasks, set deadlines, and track progress efficiently. JavaScript frameworks like React or Angular, along with libraries like Redux or Vuex, are often used to create interactive interfaces for managing tasks and collaborating with team members.

JavaScript is used to implement features such as task creation, editing, and deletion, as well as drag-and-drop functionality for reordering tasks. Real-time synchronization with backend servers, implemented using technologies like WebSocket or HTTP polling, ensures that changes are immediately reflected across all devices.

4. Interactive Data Visualization

JavaScript is also widely employed in building interactive data visualization tools, which enable users to explore and analyze complex datasets through visual representations. Libraries like D3.js or Chart.js provide robust capabilities for creating charts, graphs, maps, and other visualizations on the web.

Developers leverage JavaScript to process and transform raw data into meaningful visualizations, allowing users to interact with the data dynamically.

Features such as zooming, panning, and filtering are implemented using JavaScript to provide users with intuitive controls for exploring the data.

5. Online Learning Platform

Online learning platforms leverage JavaScript to deliver engaging and interactive educational experiences to users. JavaScript frameworks like React or Vue.js are used to create course interfaces, quizzes, and interactive exercises that facilitate learning.

JavaScript is employed to track user progress, handle quiz submissions, and provide feedback in real-time. Integration with video streaming services like YouTube or Vimeo allows for the delivery of video content, while JavaScript is used to enhance the user interface with features like progress tracking and bookmarking.

6. Content Management System (CMS)

Content management systems (CMS) enable users to create, manage, and publish digital content on the web. JavaScript frameworks like Next.js or Nuxt.js are often employed to build CMS applications with server-side rendering (SSR) or static site generation (SSG) capabilities for improved performance and SEO.

JavaScript is utilized to implement features such as content editing, version control, and user authentication. Rich text editors like Draft.js or Quill.js are integrated using JavaScript to provide users with intuitive tools for creating and formatting content.

By studying these case studies, developers can gain insights into how JavaScript can be applied to solve real-world problems and build innovative solutions that meet the needs of users across various domains. JavaScript's versatility and adaptability make it a valuable tool for developing a wide range of applications, from e-commerce platforms to social media dashboards and beyond.

Conclusion

In summary, the "Certified Web Developer: Novice To Ninja" book bundle provides a comprehensive and structured learning path for individuals aspiring to become proficient web developers. Through the three books included in this bundle, namely "HTML Essentials: Building Blocks of the Web," "Mastering CSS: Styling Techniques for Professional Web Design," and "JavaScript Wizardry: Advanced Techniques for Dynamic Web Development," readers are equipped with the essential knowledge and skills needed to excel in the field of web development.

Book 1, "HTML Essentials," serves as a solid foundation by introducing readers to the fundamental building blocks of the web - HTML. Readers learn how to structure web pages effectively, create semantic markup, and incorporate various HTML elements to build well-structured and accessible websites.

In Book 2, "Mastering CSS," readers delve into the realm of Cascading Style Sheets (CSS) and learn advanced styling techniques to enhance the visual appeal and user experience of their websites. From understanding the box model to implementing responsive design principles, readers gain expertise in crafting professional and aesthetically pleasing web interfaces.

Book 3, "JavaScript Wizardry," elevates readers' skills to the next level by exploring advanced techniques for dynamic web development using JavaScript. From manipulating the Document Object Model (DOM) to handling asynchronous operations and implementing modern JavaScript frameworks, readers acquire the proficiency needed to create interactive and feature-rich web applications.

Together, these three books cover the essential pillars of web development - HTML, CSS, and JavaScript - and provide readers with the knowledge and tools necessary to embark on a successful career journey as certified web developers. Whether you are a novice seeking to enter the field or a seasoned developer looking to expand your skill set, the "Certified Web Developer: Novice To Ninja" book bundle equips you with the expertise to thrive in the dynamic world of web development.